D0742302

THE RISE OF THE GLOBAL MIDDLE CLASS

How the Search for the Good Life Can Change the World

HOMI KHARAS

BROOKINGS INSTITUTION PRESS
Washington, D.C.

Published by Brookings Institution Press
1775 Massachusetts Avenue, NW
Washington, DC 20036
www.brookings.edu/bipress

Co-published by Rowman & Littlefield
An imprint of The Rowman & Littlefield Publishing Group, Inc.
4501 Forbes Boulevard, Suite 200, Lanham, Maryland 20706
www.rowman.com

86-90 Paul Street, London EC2A 4NE

Distributed by NATIONAL BOOK NETWORK

British Library Cataloguing in Publication Information Available

Library of Congress Cataloging-in-Publication Data

Names: Kharas, Homi J., 1954– author.
Title: The rise of the global middle class : how the search for the good life can change the world / Homi Kharas.
Description: Washington, D.C. : Brookings Institution Press, [2024] | Includes bibliographical references and index.
Identifiers: LCCN 2023017061 (print) | LCCN 2023017062 (ebook) | ISBN 9780815740322 (cloth ; alk. paper) | ISBN 9780815740339 (ebook)
Subjects: LCSH: Middle class—History. | Economic development—History.
Classification: LCC HT684 .K478 2024 (print) | LCC HT684 (ebook) | DDC 305.5/509—dc23/eng/20230421
LC record available at https://lccn.loc.gov/2023017061
LC ebook record available at https://lccn.loc.gov/2023017062

∞™ The paper used in this publication meets the minimum requirements of American National Standard for Information Sciences—Permanence of Paper for Printed Library Materials, ANSI/NISO Z39.48-1992.

CONTENTS

PREFACE
The Good Life

The good life is the end [purpose] of the city-state.

—Aristotle, ca. 330 BC

If you are reading this book, chances are that you belong to the global middle class and are enjoying what Aristotle called "the good life." For two millennia, policymakers have been trying to expand the size of the middle class, but until two centuries ago they were largely unsuccessful because any economic growth simply resulted in more people, not richer people. In Aristotle's time, there were about 150 million humans in the world. Around 1820, when the story of the middle class really starts, there were about 1.1 billion people. Ninety percent of them, just under one billion people, lived in extreme poverty; their lives were "solitary, poor, nasty, brutish, and short," as the seventeenth-century philosopher Thomas Hobbes put it.[1] Most of the rest were near poor. Less than 1 percent of the population—around eight million people—could be considered middle class or rich.

It was not until the early to mid-1800s that the group of people who could aspire to enjoy the good life—a group best described as a global middle class—began to grow. This group started in Europe, expanded to North America, Oceania, and Japan, and is now growing rapidly in developing countries, especially in Asia. In 2023, at the time of this writing, even though the middle class is under stress in Europe and the United States, it is expanding faster on a global scale than it has ever done before, albeit with a hiatus as countries respond to the

COVID-19 pandemic. The world has already passed a tipping point wherein half the population—four billion people—is middle class or wealthier.[2] From now on, as the middle class continues to grow, the rate of increase will decline simply because there will be fewer people who are not already in the middle class, even allowing for the fact that the global population is still growing.

In a few years' time, probably around 2030, the five billionth person will join the middle class. By then, in just two centuries, the middle class will have evolved from a group with absolutely no political power to one that dominates politics and economic policy almost everywhere. This book is the story about how the social order of the world is being transformed, about the tensions and contradictions inherent in the expansion of the middle class, and about what this may mean for the economic, social, and political fate of future generations.

Many people as individuals identify with the middle class and even prefer to be part of the middle class rather than rich or poor. Almost no one wants to be poor, although there are a few who take a vow of poverty, often accompanied by a vow of chastity and a vow of obedience. Most people do not voluntarily choose that life.

At the other end of the scale, being rich is not necessarily that appealing, and many people who are rich by objective standards self-identify with the middle class rather than the rich because they want to be considered hard-working and self-made rather than lucky, idle, and self-indulgent, adjectives often associated with those born into rich families. Social scientists have documented dozens of stories of "lucky" lottery winners who end up miserable after hitting the jackpot—so many, in fact, that there is a special term for the situation, the "curse of the lottery." The money socially isolates winners and makes them suspicious of others' motives. The winners' children are more likely to suffer from depression and anxiety. Substance abuse and even suicide increases. Moving beyond anecdotes, a study of 1.7 million people found that life satisfaction actually declines among families whose income exceeds $95,000, as does the emotional well-being among those earning more than $75,000.[3] It may sound far-fetched to think that one's well-being falls with higher income—and in truth, there is no consensus on this in academic circles—but a majority would probably agree with the core idea that money cannot buy happiness after a certain point.

For most people, the middle is a good place to be, with all the satisfaction that comes from having a fulfilling job and a life surrounded by family and friends. That is why building a large middle class has become the central economic platform of politicians in Western democracies. President Bill Clinton's political strategists James Carville and Stan Greenberg summed up their boss's economic priorities simply in their bestseller: *It's the Middle Class, Stupid!*[4] In a more academic vein, economists have argued that there is an interdependency between the middle class and economic growth. Although growth provides the jobs and wages to support a thriving middle class, the presence of a solid middle class creates growth by nurturing innovators and entrepreneurs; Thomas Edison, Bill Gates, and Steve Jobs were all born into American middle-class families. Middle-class spending also provides the demand for the new products that fuel growth. A reasonable description of the entire last two hundred years of economic history in the United States and Europe is that middle-class-centered growth created a long cycle of prosperity for entire nations.[5]

The societal benefits of a large middle class stretch beyond economics. In the Western world (Europe and English-speaking advanced economies), members of the middle class share many common values that support democracy over authoritarianism. Political scientists Ronald Inglehart and Christian Welzel suggest that Western middle-class societies prefer democracies that promote self-expression, tolerance, diversity, and environmental protection. More authoritarian societies favor traditional family values, deference to authority, and the promise of physical security. Boiled down, the Western middle class believes in individual achievement and self-reliance obtained through hard work, honesty, thrift, and perseverance and is fiercely resistant to efforts to make it subservient to the state, whereas more traditional societies place greater emphasis on strengthening the state itself.[6]

The economic success of the West compared to other regions since the early nineteenth century has been called the Great Divergence. It resulted in a global middle class that was heavily concentrated in these Western countries. In the 1980s, this was replaced by the Great Convergence, in which developing countries, especially in Asia, began to catch up to the living standards in advanced economies. One might think this is a pretty good outcome for the world. If a large middle class was good for the Western world for two hundred years, why wouldn't it be good for the whole world? Anyone writing a book like this one in 1975 would almost certainly have said that a world with five billion middle-class people would be a wonderful world compared to an alternative world where most people remain poor and vulnerable. But today the perspective is different. Why?

One reason is that scale matters, which means that more of a good thing is not always good. The global middle class is associated with consumerism, and at its current and prospective scale, it demands the production of ever more material goods and services at the cheapest possible prices. This has left in its wake massive loss of biodiversity and species extinction, crashing global fisheries, unprecedented levels of carbon emissions, depleted soils, and rain forest destruction. There is a threat of recurring pandemics as humans come into closer contact with animals. Coronaviruses, like the severe acute respiratory syndrome (SARS) outbreak in 2003, the Middle East respiratory syndrome (MERS) in 2012, and the COVID-19 pandemic in 2020 underline the fragility of a global economy driven to satisfy middle-class demands. All the data shows that planetary boundaries have been reached in several areas and that humankind needs a new model of sustainable economic growth. What is unknown is if people can invent or transition to a world economy that can support a vast global middle class without breaching the limits of what the planet can tolerate.

A second reason is that there is less confidence that a middle-class lifestyle makes everyone happier. If the purpose of politics is to deliver on what makes people happy, then the old approach of the past several decades of concentrating on the economy and growing the middle class may no longer be enough or even the most relevant way forward. In the United States, the General Social Survey has been asking the same question since 1973: "Taken all together, how would you say things are these days—would you say that you are very happy, pretty happy, or not too happy?" The results for adults show a steep decline since the late 1980s, even though the US middle class is among the largest and richest in the world.[7] As a general proposition, being part of the middle class in the West is no longer seen as a ticket to happiness and well-being. If anything, fears about losing middle-class status for themselves or their children are stoking worries and even deaths due to despair—mortality resulting from suicide, opioids, and alcohol—among white men and women without a college degree in the United States, as well as deaths due to exhaustion in the case of male workers in Japan.[8] So simply having a larger middle class in the world can no longer be equated with having a better world. There are nonmaterial aspects of being middle class, like mental health, that contribute to life satisfaction and emotional well-being, which are taking center stage in many advanced countries, and these have been neglected for too long by governments.

What's true for the individual is also true for whole societies. A huge middle class has not saved the European or Japanese economies from decades of stagnation and poor growth. Nationalism, racism, xenophobia, and declining trust in almost all institutions seem to be resurfacing across the Western middle class, so it is hard to argue convincingly that a middle-class background is the key to a good life in the Western world.[9] A book by economists Eric Lonergan and Mark Blyth, aptly titled *Angrynomics*, describes the disconnect between people's lived experiences in the Western world and the economic data showing growing prosperity.[10]

A third reason for thinking anew is that the global middle class no longer seems to share its values across borders. The idea that middle-class societies are fundamentally peaceful and democratic has given way to worries in some Western countries that a new middle class, found in countries in Asia, Eastern Europe, and Latin America, represents a challenge rather than a source of growing mutual prosperity.

The new middle class that has spread so rapidly in Asia and other developing countries looks to be quite different from the Western middle class. Back in the 1950s, the American sociologist Seymour Martin Lipset argued that democracies flourish when there is economic development (industrialization, wealth, urbanization, and education, all of which are also drivers of a middle class) and institutions that most citizens (read: the middle class) considered legitimate.[11] The analysis raised hopes that a large middle class would promote democracy wherever it took root. However, the link between democracy and the middle class appears weak, and several of the countries with the largest new middle classes, like China, Turkey, and Iran, show no signs of becoming more democratic. Even in more democratic countries, such as Hungary, Poland, Brazil, and India, the middle class is turning against the very protections for minorities that are considered the hallmarks of liberal democracy. The nongovernmental organization (NGO) Freedom House has recorded global declines in civil liberties and political rights for thirteen consecutive years. It classifies most of East and Southeast Asia and many other emerging economies as "not free," even though their middle class has been expanding at a rapid pace.

This matters because the global middle class no longer consists primarily of the middle class in Western economies. The shift in the balance between the Western and Asian middle class during this century has been dramatic, with rapid convergence happening during the two most recent crises: the Great Recession of 2008 and 2009, which is called the North Atlantic Financial Crisis in Asia (underscoring how little Asian countries were affected) and the COVID-19 pandemic that began in 2020.

During the Great Recession, the fortunes of the Western middle class collapsed. In 2009, unemployment in the United States and Europe spiked and wages fell at alarming rates. Annual personal consumption expenditures fell by $160 billion in the United States between 2008 and 2009.[12] To put this in perspective, annual consumption in the United States had fallen only once since World War II, after the first oil shock in 1974, and that was quickly followed by a rebound the next year. In Europe, consumption levels in 2009 started on a downward path that still had not regained previous levels ten years later. The crisis wiped out financial savings for many middle-class households.[13]

The same is happening again as countries respond to COVID-19. The Western middle class took a hard hit in 2020 and 2021 as economic growth and consumption fell. Rising inequality added to middle-class woes. In 2020, the United States saw unemployment at levels like those during the Great Depression, and every advanced economy fell into recession, despite unprecedented economic support programs by governments and central banks.

On the other side of the world, governments in Asia have managed global crises much better. They pumped money into their economies through tax cuts and expanded public works to create domestic demand to offset the impact of the Great Recession. This created jobs and lifted wages to support the middle class. These actions turbocharged a preexisting trend, as the middle class was already growing in Asia. An Asian middle class that had long been present in Japan, Taiwan, Hong Kong, South Korea, and Singapore spread like wildfire after 2010 to include billions of people inhabiting East Asia and the Indian subcontinent.

Asian countries, particularly India, have also been hit by the COVID-19 pandemic, but East Asia had some of the most aggressive and successful initial responses. Many Asian countries had a trial run with SARS in 2003, and based on that experience, they set up protocols for testing, quarantining, and contact tracing that were rapidly deployed to combat COVID-19. This permitted them to contain the spread of the disease and to expand their economies more rapidly than other countries.

Looking forward and assuming continued success with combating COVID-19, around one hundred million Asian citizens are joining the middle class each year. Total spending by Asian middle-class households is already as large as spending by North Americans in current dollars, 50 percent more than by Europeans, and more than both Europe and North America combined when adjusted for the lower prevailing prices in Asia. And the Asian middle-class majority is poised to continue to grow.

Almost nine out of ten new entrants to the global middle class will be Asian, so the chances are very high that an Asian will be the five billionth member of the global middle class.[14] It is no exaggeration to say that the growth of the global middle class and its tilt toward Asia could be the most significant megatrend of this era. The middle class has affected every aspect of life in the West, so it is reasonable to suppose that it will deeply affect non-Western countries too.

The big question is whether the political, economic, and social features of the middle class are stable over time and across geographies or whether they are shifting. One needs to ask: Is growing the middle class good or bad for individuals, for society, and for the planet? It is a question full of contradictions and complexities. Will a larger global middle class bring about more happiness for more people or will it create more unhappiness because of worries about competition among the middle classes of different countries? Will middle-class consumerism pressure companies to adopt more responsible environmental and social practices or will the pressure of competition to deliver cheap goods force companies to ignore safe planetary limits on carbon emissions, biodiversity, and nitrogen use, which could trigger unpredictable consequences? Will middle-class societies choose democracy or some alternative form of government to deliver stability and order? Will the next generation seek to become middle class or reject it as a rat race toward materialism and stress?

The answers to these questions have consequences for humanity that are too important to ignore. They will drive the way people think and act regarding globalization, technology, politics, and economic policies. As with all big questions, it is hard to know where to begin to think about them seriously. Defining the middle class seems like a good place to start. This is what the first chapter of this book is about. Chapter 2 discusses the emergence of the first billion people in the middle class, largely in the West. Chapter 3 describes where the next billion middle class cohort came from, a mix of Eastern Europe after the fall of the Berlin Wall, Latin America, and East Asian miracle economies. Chapter 4 turns to China, which accounted for most of the third billion in the middle class, and chapter 5 reviews how India came to make such a large contribution to the fourth billion. Sadly, Africa is not part of this story. Despite the fact that the continent has more than one billion people, its middle-class population is still small in terms of global trends. A few African countries, including Egypt, Tunisia, and perhaps Botswana have majority middle-class societies, but most countries on the continent have a middle class of less than 10 percent of their population.

Though economic growth is undoubtedly a large part of the story, looking at the development of the middle class requires a perspective on growth and the pattern of growth—who gains, who does not; whether jobs and wages rise or profits do. Chapter 6 peers into the future and outlines the obstacles in the way of adding a fifth billion to the middle class by 2030. Chapter 7 concludes by sketching an outline of a new policy agenda that could improve the well-being of the world's potential five-billion-strong middle-class group.

~

Chapter 1

THE MIDDLING SORT

> Mine was the middle state . . . the best state in the world, the most suited to human happiness, not exposed to the miseries and hardships . . . of the mechanick part of mankind, and not embarrassed with the pride, luxury, ambition, and envy of the upper part of mankind.
>
> —Daniel Defoe, *Robinson Crusoe*, 1719

When Charles Henry Harrod opened a shop in West London, England, in 1849, he was hoping to capitalize on the excitement of the upcoming Great Exhibition of the Works of Industry of All Nations to be held in nearby Hyde Park. This first-ever world's fair showed off the wonders of new technologies and machinery, musical and scientific instruments of all kinds, and arts and crafts, all housed within the magnificent "Crystal Palace." The exhibition underscored Britain's leadership in the Industrial Revolution and drew six million visitors, most paying the cheapest admission fee of 1 shilling for a weekday pass (about £5 in today's currency).[1]

Across the English Channel, Aristide Boucicaut revamped his department store, Le Bon Marché, in 1852 in a way that revolutionized shopping. In the mid-nineteenth century, most people went to outdoor markets, haggled with vendors over prices, and hoped for the best in terms of quality and variety. The rich, of course, simply summoned tradesmen to their houses. What Le Bon Marché offered was a new experience. It made available a large variety of goods at fixed prices in a clean and safe physical space. It also advertised its wares to introduce customers to new products.[2]

What Harrod and Boucicaut had anticipated was that there was a brand-new type of customer to be served in the mid-nineteenth century, a middling sort of person who was neither a member of the nobility nor a peasant—someone who had enough spare cash to afford an experience like a visit to the world's fair and who could be persuaded to spend some of that cash on goods he or she had never experienced before. With hindsight, it turns out they were right.

The Origins of the Middle Class

In the mid-nineteenth century, it was quite simple to sort people according to their social class. Their incomes, dress, and even accents set them apart. But as societies grew more complex, it became necessary to standardize a definition of the middle class to understand its development over time.

According to the *Encyclopedia Britannica*, a social class is "a group of people within a society who possess the same socioeconomic status." However, there is no universal definition of what this means precisely. "Socioeconomic status" can be defined by income, wealth, consumption, aspirations, position in the social hierarchy, or opportunity. A social class can be constructed in terms of what people have in common or in terms of what differentiates them from others.

The idea of a social class is itself a comparatively modern phenomenon. In the eighteenth century, writers describing the society of their time used words like "the people" or "the laboring poor" to categorize those who were hierarchically subservient to the dominant group, who professed to be in their ruling position as part of a divine design.[3]

At the beginning of the nineteenth century, people were divided into the aristocracy, who largely derived their wealth from owning and renting out large tracts of land that they or their ancestors had acquired by force, and peasants, who worked on the land. It was simple to distinguish between these groups, and there was almost no mobility between them, so there was little need to separate them into "classes."

This started to change with the emergence of a new group, initially called the "bourgeoisie," a word derived from the old French for "town dweller." The bourgeoisie were urbanites who made their livelihood from the new world of manufacturing and the services that supported it, such as trade, banking, and accounting. Merchants were among the early members of the bourgeoisie, relying on capital to buy things produced in foreign places, transport them back home, and then sell them domestically. Great fortunes could be made or lost through trade.

The most famous example of this was the rise and fall of the tulip market in Holland. The Dutch were the most successful traders in Europe, and a middle class was starting to emerge in Holland as early as the seventeenth century. Dutch traders found a flower in Turkey that was quite different from anything growing on the European continent. The tulip was something exotic and scarce and also visible to one's neighbors. It quickly became a status good in Holland, an early example of something that the American sociologist Thorstein Veblen would later classify as a symbol of conspicuous consumption.[4] In Veblen's analysis, demand for a status good could rise when the price went up, because possession or consumption demonstrated wealth in an obvious way. This behavior contradicted the usual economics of supply and demand, and it generated unstable markets. This is exactly what happened to the Dutch tulip market between 1634 and 1637. Prices soared to impossible levels, with a single bulb costing the equivalent of a mansion on the Amsterdam Grand Canal. By the end of 1637, prices had crashed, causing bankruptcies and a collapse in confidence and social trust.

The Dutch tulip bubble is a cautionary tale about market imperfections and the "popular delusions and the madness of crowds," as the Scottish journalist Charles Mackay would write in the mid-nineteenth century.[5] But it is also a tale that could not have been told without a middle class. It was the proto-middle class in Holland that created the huge demand for tulips and drove prices to exorbitant levels. Bankers were prepared to extend credit to members of the middle class to purchase bulbs and set up bulb trading companies. The middle class was the group that either possessed the "wisdom of markets" or else suffered from the madness of crowds. It drew its power from the sheer number of people that belonged to it.

It is this notion of size and the power to affect society that creates a socioeconomic class. The German sociologist Max Weber wrote about the different ways that an individual could acquire or wield power. It could come from the political order, by birth into the nobility, by access to economic wealth, or by personal status or prestige conferred by society on great scientists, priests, or artists. Though these routes to power could overlap, there were also clear boundaries. In Europe, many Jewish families were wealthy but had little political power. They would never be considered upper class. Conversely, many members of the minor rural aristocracy were not wealthy but enjoyed access to the royal court. They could be upper class even without wealth.

Nevertheless, most of the time, class was closely linked to both the size and origin of one's income. Aristocrats and royalty derived their wealth from their large land holdings. Peasants and workers relied on manual labor as their main source of income. In the middle were those who used capital to make money—such as traders, bankers, and manufacturers—alongside a group using what is now called human capital or education, including lawyers, doctors, clerics, and teachers.

These three groups became the three classes that today are called the upper class, the working (or lower) class, and the middle class. This stratification became so common that the British philosopher John Stuart Mill felt the need to remind his peers that class was an invention of humans, not God: "Social commentators revolve in their eternal circle of landlords, capitalists and labourers, until they seem to think of the distinction of society into those three classes as if it were one of God's ordinances, not man's, and as little under human control as the division of day and night."[6]

Conveniently, in the nineteenth century, the composition of the three major classes was the same, regardless of whether the classification was based on social status or on income. Sometimes these classes were subdivided into additional groups, like upper-middle class and lower-middle class, with distinct characteristics, but broadly speaking, a three-tier classification has been used for more than two centuries.

The coincidence that there are three social groups—aristocracy, bourgeoisie, and peasants/workers—and three sources of income—

land, capital, and labor—is an oversimplification of the idea that class and income sources overlap. The dividing lines for each group do not always correspond exactly. To illustrate, the upper classes derived considerable income from banking and capital as well as from land, often using their political power to ensure success. The South Sea Company in England (the company at the heart of the infamous South Sea Bubble of 1720, the world's first financial crisis) is a good example. It was granted monopoly trading rights with Latin America in the eighteenth century, and King George I became its governor. Both aristocrats and bankers looked to it as a source of easy wealth.

As another example of fluid class boundaries, some countries allowed rich merchants to buy themselves a title. In eighteenth-century France, provincial gentlemen were slowly being displaced in their national social hierarchy by the centralization of power in the hands of the royal court. These lesser noblemen found it advantageous to sell their titles and fiefs to richer people who basically bought the prestige of belonging to the upper class—something that money alone did not confer. In the court of Louis XIV, the titular rank (and the associated hierarchy status) was literally measured by its weight in gold—there were different types and grades of nobility and each had its own price.[7]

There was also socioeconomic mobility between the lower and middle classes. Charles Dickens's *David Copperfield* weaves together personal experiences and fiction in a rags-to-riches (or at least rags-to-happiness) story. The young Dickens was poor, and as a young boy, he worked in a warehouse. His father was thrown in jail for penury and failure to repay his debts when Charles was just nine years old. By the time he died in 1870, Dickens was one of the most famous people in Britain. He was buried in Poets' Corner in Westminster Abbey, and his wife received personal condolences from Queen Victoria. Dickens was able to move from lower to middle class, but for all his fame and fortune, he would never have been considered upper class in England, nor would he have wanted to be thought of in that way. His preference (which was disregarded) was to be buried in a small graveyard in a little church close to his country home, a very typical middle-class aspiration.[8]

Defining the Middle Class: The Ability to Live the Good Life

Any definition of class in nineteenth-century European societies must confront the rigidity of perceptions of the class structure while also allowing for the considerable social mobility of individuals between classes. Having a rigid definition of class is useful in identifying broad trends in the size of each class, as well as the rise and fall of movements that drive societal change. It is less useful when considering any specific individual's experiences and opportunities—how to classify a poor nobleman or a rich farmer can be subjective and context specific.

Looking at the origins of the middle class suggests that it was initially distinguished from other classes through occupations—including salaried wage earners, the clergy, military officers, and bankers, lawyers, traders, and accountants. Later on, teachers, doctors, nurses, and civil servants would add to the count of the middle class.

The incomes earned from these occupations also distinguished the middle class from other classes—substantially lower than the incomes of the upper class and substantially higher than the incomes of peasants and day laborers. For example, a junior clerk in a bank in London in 1850 made £90 to £100 a year (about £15,900 in today's money). With this, he could afford to rent and furnish a small cottage, and his wife could employ at least one servant (for about £6 a year plus room and board).[9] Even if he became chairman of the bank board, with a salary of £1,000, he would still be middle class. The upper class, the landed gentry that had agricultural land to rent out to tenant farmers, would have incomes of at least £60,000 to £100,000 per year. The very wealthy, like the Marquess of Westminster, might have had an income topping £1 million per year.[10]

It would be a mistake, however, to define the middle class in purely economic terms. The power and prestige of the middle class has always come from its economic importance, but, as the emerging art form of the Victorian novel would show, the middle class also had a distinct set of values and social behaviors. Members of the middle class spent their money in ways that were different from those of the other classes, as

Harrod and Boucicaut discovered. And when the middle class did not have enough money, they could get credit, as the tulip mania illustrated.

The Victorian middle-class ideal followed the original thinking of Aristotle and the Greek philosophers. Aristotle believed that eudaemonia, loosely translated as "the good life," was the most desirable state, but he also acknowledged that there was substantial disagreement as to exactly what this meant. Eudaemonia consisted of living well and doing things well, a pursuit of excellence in all activities.

For the Greeks, the main way of achieving eudaemonia was the path of exercising virtue, the ultimate end in itself. All other household attributes, like occupation, income, and spending, were merely a means of achieving happiness. Even Epicurus—the fourth-century BC Greek philosopher most associated with hedonism or the pursuit of material pleasures—emphasized the importance of friendship, study, and inner harmony. Each of these could be measured as positive subjective experiences, so the good life could then be construed as having as many pleasurable experiences as possible.

The Greeks put great weight on living a life of generosity, justice, friendship, and citizenship, while recognizing that this required sufficient access to material goods. Having power was less important to the Greeks. In fact, Epicurus felt that politics should be avoided whenever possible and that politicians could only rarely aspire to a good life.

Fast forward from the Greeks to the Victorians. The main Greek ideas of trying to pursue the good life in both material and emotional ways had been passed down by a series of philosophers, including Saint Thomas Aquinas in the thirteenth century. But the good life was hard to achieve in practice without freedom from poverty and mental anxiety. Most of the population in the early nineteenth century had miserable lives and lived in abject poverty. They could not aspire to the good life.

At the other end of the social scale, the aristocracy had to deal with court intrigue and power politics, sometimes consolidated through rather unpleasant tactics including inbreeding and murder. At the start of the nineteenth century, European aristocrats were trembling in the shadow of the French Revolution.

In this environment, the middle class stood out as a distinctive group who could aspire to the good life in a way that was not possible for either the upper class or the working class. They were rich enough to enjoy material comforts, they enjoyed some leisure and vacations, but they were not so rich as to be in danger of having their heads chopped off.

Measuring the Middle Class

The definition of the middle class as comprising households that aspire to live the good life is conceptual rather than quantitative. To measure the size of the middle class, one needs to transform the concepts of class into something numerical. This is no easy matter, since classifying people into classes is subjective; the middle class seems to fall into the category of things that are hard to define but that most people can recognize when they see it. A middle-class household has certain observable characteristics—it is not poor and has sufficient means that a single economic shock (say, a spell of unemployment or sickness) would not thrust it into poverty. At the same time, a middle-class household is not rich in the sense of being totally free of economic anxiety. Of course, although income is one attribute that can be used to draw boundaries between lower, middle, and upper classes, other attributes also can be considered and will result in different classifications. Because of this, there will be gray areas at the boundaries of the classes. If the classes are broad, however, then most people will not be very close to a boundary regardless of the attribute used, and the size of each class can still be measured with some confidence.

The approach I use in this book is simple. Imagine placing everyone in a society in a long line in order of their class status as defined by some attribute or set of attributes. Then identify a lower boundary and call all those people falling below this boundary "lower class." Move on and define an upper boundary, and call all the people above that "upper class." The middle class is then defined as those in between. With this approach, the challenge is not to define the middle class directly, but to define the lower class and the upper class, with the middle class representing everyone else.

There are two important steps to this process that make it less straightforward than it might seem. The first step is to choose a single attribute or indicator from a group of attributes that describes the social hierarchy. There is considerable evidence that hierarchies exist among animals that live in groups, that these hierarchies form spontaneously, and that they are useful for the group as a whole. Among humans, hierarchies can be multidimensional in terms of power (control over resources), influence (allocation of resources), or dominance (ability to acquire resources), so being in the middle of the hierarchy along one dimension may not necessarily mean being in the middle of the hierarchy on another dimension. This is one reason why many academics prefer to talk about several middle classes rather than a single middle class. However, there is enough overlap so that using a single dimension to describe the social hierarchy still permits a good approximation of the overall social order of individuals within a group. Once this is done, the logical second step is to define boundary limits along this indicator to separate between the working and middle classes and between the middle and upper classes.

The most commonly used sorting indicator of class today is the level of household income, preferably adjusted for family size and cost-of-living price differences across locations. This is certainly what was important to the Victorians. What really separated people in the nineteenth century was how much they earned, and there were clear gaps in income at each boundary between the working and middle classes as well as between the middle and upper classes. Even the language and use of words like "poor" and "rich" to denote those in the lower and upper classes relate the notions of income and class to each other. An additional attraction of income as an indicator is that data are readily available going back hundreds of years from official surveys, wage records, and filings of taxpayers.

The problem is that looking just at income does not always capture the essence of the middle-class experience today, because income is only one of many variables that affect one's living standards. Government assistance, savings, inheritance, credit, capital gains, and asset sales are other ways of getting money that are now available on a far greater scale than was possible in the nineteenth century.

As an example of how this can make a difference, imagine two college students—one from a poor family who is working her way through college, the other from a middle-class household whose parents are paying her tuition and who does not have a job. On an income basis, the former would be ranked above the latter and more likely to be classified as middle class. But common sense would suggest the opposite. In addition, household incomes tend to vary quite a bit from year to year, especially for the self-employed and small business owners. Class, on the other hand, is a more stable concept. Thus, it is problematic to use an indicator like income that would result in households frequently moving in and out of the middle class.

For this reason, some scholars prefer to use wealth as a metric. Credit Suisse, the financial services company, defines the global middle class as adults owning between $10,000 and $100,000 in net assets, including housing. Above this range, Credit Suisse classifies households as high net worth.[11] But wealth, too, has its drawbacks: the Great Recession of 2008 was caused by a sharp contraction in housing prices that sent wealth levels plummeting in many advanced economies, only for them to recover equally rapidly in the following years. And the wealth of individual households is not readily available for the nineteenth century, making wealth difficult to use in a historical study.

An alternative to both income and wealth is to conceive of the middle class in terms of how much people spend. This is the sorting indicator I use in this book. Household expenditures are closely linked to what economists call "permanent income," the income that people believe they will enjoy over their lifespan and that best reflects their standard of living. To return to the example of the two students: the one from a poor household might not be eating out in restaurants and taking trips abroad during the summer. She would be working and saving. The other student, from the middle-class household, might have the option of spending more if her parents provide an allowance. Neither are likely to be earning a lot, but by looking at their expenditures, they could be classified into their respective classes in a more accurate way than by looking at their incomes.

An expenditure indicator also helps in comparing households headed by individuals of different ages and stages of life. Most people borrow when they are young, taking advantage of mortgages, credit cards, and car and other personal loans. They save and pay off these debts during their prime working age. When they are old and retired, they may not have much income, but can consume their savings. Retirees should still be classified as middle class, even if their retirement incomes are low. In general, household spending is much steadier over time than income or even wealth, so spending provides a convenient metric for sorting households from top to bottom.

Relative versus Absolute Definitions of Class Boundaries

Once a sorting indicator has been chosen, what remains is to establish the boundaries that separate the classes. There has been debate about how to set these boundaries for more than two centuries now, with no established consensus.

Boundaries can be quite arbitrary, with little to distinguish those just on one side from those just on the other side, but they are a useful simplifying device to make choices about classification of households. Ordering everyone in society is a highly subjective task anyway because there are so many dimensions along which people differ. So it is easy to understand why boundaries between classes should not be taken as hard and fast rules.

There are two basic lines of thinking as to how to define the boundaries of the middle class, each with its strengths and weaknesses. One compares individuals with others in the same society—a relative approach—whereas the other uses fixed values for the boundaries—an absolute approach. The relative approach compares a household with others to assess whether it is middle class; the absolute approach looks only at each household itself. To illustrate, the Pew Research Center uses a relative way to define the middle class in the United States; it classifies as middle class all those who have two-thirds to twice the national median income among households of the same size. To apply this definition, one needs information about the household being classified, as well as about the national median income and its distribution. Hence, this definition follows in the tradition of "keeping up with the Joneses," a psychological sense of being a member of the same economic group as one's neighbors. The implication, however, is that if the benchmark of median income changes, a household maintaining the same level of income over time could appear richer or poorer and even change classification without any changes to its own spending. Under a relative definition like this, being in the middle class would no longer reflect the ability to buy enough to pursue the good life in the sense used by the ancient Greeks. It would only indicate how a household is doing compared to the chosen benchmark.

The absolute approach—the method I use in this book—sets a fixed spending range to identify whether a household should be classified as middle class or not. The range is adjusted for household size, for the changing value of money due to inflation over time within any country, and for price differences across countries. Households with expenditures below a certain level are defined as lower class, those with expenditures above another level are defined as rich, and the middle class is everyone in between. In this example of absolute boundaries, a household can be sorted into its class with no information about other households.

There are some advantages to an absolute boundary. There is no need to define the relevant comparator. Does someone living in New York really believe his or her class should be affected by the fact that there are relatively poor people living in Mississippi? Wouldn't it be inconsistent if an Italian household was defined as being in Italy's middle class but not in a European middle class? Do we want to designate a household making an average income in Burundi, one of the world's poorest countries, as middle class, even if its absolute spending power adjusted for the price difference across countries is so much lower than a poor household in Singapore? The use of absolute boundaries avoids these oddities.

The difference between employing an absolute or a relative definition of the middle class is not simply an academic exercise. It can have real consequences. Nestlé, the largest food and beverage company in the world, decided on a major expansion into Africa in 2008, in part because of an analysis done by the African Development Bank suggesting that there were 330 million middle-class Africans. By 2015, Nestlé was forced to slash its workforce in Africa because the middle-class consumption there had been so disappointing; the company cited an alternative estimate of the African middle class of eleven million people, done by Standard Bank.[12] The difference: the African Development Bank had used a relative definition of the middle class, but this group still had so little purchasing power that it could not afford Nestlé products. From Nestlé's standpoint of identifying potential customers, the absolute definition used by Standard Bank was more relevant.

Having decided to use absolute boundaries to define the middle class, what remains is to set appropriate values for the thresholds demarcating the lower/middle and the middle/upper boundaries. There are various ways of doing this, but luckily the different methods tend to produce similar results. This provides a reasonable measure of robustness to the boundaries.

One method is to identify the spending of a person at the bottom of the middle class, the least well-off entrant into this class. In Victorian England, this was a junior clerk. If one sets the middle-class boundary as his (and it was always a man in those days) expenditure, one can calculate the boundary value separating the lower and middle class. Historical records show that a clerk spent about £100 a year, or £15,910 in today's currency (after adjusting for inflation).[13] That is equivalent to $22,700 per year, or $62 per day when adjusted for cost-of-living differences between the United Kingdom and the United States.[14] This figure also needs to be adjusted to account for household size. A reasonable approximation for a young family in nineteenth-century England would be five people, yielding a middle-class lower boundary of about $12 per person per day in today's US dollars, adjusted for price differences across countries and over time. Ideally, the adjustment for price differentials would be made by regions and cities within a country as well, but this is too complex a task given the data at hand. It serves, however, as a reminder that the measures being used are imperfect approximations that are consistent over time and space, even if not perfectly accurate in any given instance.

Coincidentally, £100 a year was also used by the mid-nineteenth-century chancellor of the exchequer, William Gladstone, as "the dividing line . . . between the educated and the labouring part of the community," which he then used to identify who would be subject to income tax.[15] So this threshold seems to reflect the class divisions of the time. In a similar vein, the American poet Walt Whitman editorialized in 1858 that "the most valuable class in any community is the middle class, the men of moderate means living at the rate of a thousand dollars a year, or thereabouts."[16] Converted into today's dollars and adjusted for the average family size of the time, 5.55 people, $1,000 represents about $11.70 per person per day.

A second method builds on the idea that being middle class means not having to worry about falling into poverty, with all that entails in terms of providing food and shelter for one's family. Most families worry about sickness, death, unemployment, or crop failures when they think about what might happen to affect their future livelihood. Recent research in Chile, Mexico, and Peru tracked the same households over time and found that those households with initial spending of more than $12 per person per day (in 2017 dollars) had only a 10 percent chance of falling into extreme poverty as a result of economic shocks in a three-year period.[17] So if the middle class is to refer to households with little chance of falling into poverty, a lower bound of at least $12 per person per day should be used.

A third method is to consider the lower boundary of the middle class as identifying those people who would not be considered poor in Portugal and Italy, the two advanced economies with the strictest definitions of poverty. The boundary calculated in this way is, again, $12 per person per day in today's terms.

The fact that each of these measures of the boundary between the middle class and the lower class is similar, despite different methods being applied in different centuries and across different continents, suggests that the boundary captures the basic concept of what it means to be middle class in very different contexts. For the Victorians, being middle class meant having the opportunity for one's family to have a better life through one's own efforts and hard work. For contemporary researchers of economic development, being middle class is being free from the imminent vulnerability of falling into poverty. For politicians in rich countries, being middle class means not being poor. Regardless of which perspective one takes, the boundary threshold is the same. Being middle class requires a household to have enough resources to spend $12 per person per day.

The upper boundary between the middle class and the upper class has received less attention, partly because so few people have crossed over this point until recently. In the research that I have drawn on for this book, I set the upper boundary at ten times the spending level of the lower boundary, at $120 per person per day.[18] This is mathematically equivalent to a spending level of $175,200 per year for a four-person household. This level of spending corresponds to the level at which at least one wealthy country, Luxembourg, defines people as rich, so it is a boundary that has been validated by current practice.

At the Core of Middle-Class Life: Living Well and Doing Things Well

The fact that the middle class can be measured by spending does not mean that spending is the only characteristic of a middle-class family. *Mrs. Beeton's Book of Household Management*, the authoritative thousand-page volume about how a middle-class household should live and behave in mid-Victorian England, was published in 1861. It is still available on Amazon.com, but readers today would not find its commentary on the niceties of silver tea services, porcelain china, or pride in light pastry relevant to contemporary life.

What has stood the test of time is the way of life that is made possible in a middle-class setting. Mrs. Beeton's book promised a better life to those who worked hard, saved, and kept themselves and their households clean.[19] One and a half centuries later, President Barack Obama established a task force on the middle class in America that came to the same conclusion: "Middle-class families are defined by their aspirations more than their income."[20] The task force went on to describe core aspects of a middle-class life: being able to afford good housing, a car, an annual vacation, and education for one's children; having security for health care and retirement; and having a balanced allocation of time for work, leisure, child care, and household chores.

The commonality between Mrs. Beeton and the Obama task force is that both describe middle-class families that can afford to live well through their own efforts and hard work. They have the freedom to choose how they spend because they have access to money, but they also have the responsibility and necessity to choose wisely because they are not rich. The details regarding what they spend their money on to live well are quite different between the nineteenth and twenty-first centuries, but the freedoms and responsibilities of choice over how they live, with a belief in thrift, saving, determination, and perseverance, are the same.

This dual nature of the middle class is important because, as a class, they look to government to provide the conditions under which the pathway to success—the good behavior from a social point of view—is appropriately rewarded. The middle class thrives in a meritocratic and fair economic system. It cannot be considered simply a segment of the population that lies between rich and poor. It is a group whose lifestyle is broadly perceived as deserved, who contribute to society as much as they benefit from the political, social, and economic order in which they live. The rich often just get lucky. They may then have to wrestle with a moral dilemma about whether they should devote their wealth to the public good or if this harms society by interfering with the "survival of the fittest" competitive structure thought to be needed for progress. The poor are often unjustly paid too little for their labor because they have no other options except to work and do whatever is needed to survive. The middle class contribute their talents and diligence to society, and society rewards them proportionately. They benefit from what they consume, from how they earn their livelihood, and from the dignity of fulfilling their personal responsibility to provide for themselves and their families through work.

For most people, membership in the middle class is therefore the most sought-after club in the world, and it has been so since the times of the ancient Greeks, if not before. Yet as late as 1830, there were probably fewer than 10 million people out of a world population of 1.1 billion who could be classified as belonging to the global middle class. The story of the next two centuries would be the story of how a class that was smaller than 1 percent of the population and that had barely expanded during two millennia could multiply by five hundred times and spread across the globe. It all started in the United Kingdom of Great Britain and Ireland, so that is where this story begins.

~

Chapter 2

THE FIRST BILLION

The Victorians and the Rise of the West, 1830–1975

> The American Dream is that dream of a land in which life should be better and richer and fuller for everyone, with opportunity for each according to ability or achievement.
>
> —James Truslow Adams, *The Epic of America*, 1931

When Queen Victoria ascended to the throne of England in 1837, there were about 1.1 billion people in the world. Three-quarters lived in Asia: 500 million in East Asia, 250 million in South Asia, and a few million in Central Asia. Europe had about 280 million people. The remainder of the world was relatively sparsely populated: perhaps 18 million people in all of North America, 32 million in sub-Saharan Africa, 27 million in Latin America, and 29 million in the Middle East and North Africa. The global number of the rich stood at around 11,000 people. Around 12 million people, or 1 percent of the global population, would have fallen into the range now considered to be middle class. Everyone else was in the lower class: extremely poor or vulnerable to falling into poverty.

The largest number of the middle class lived in Europe—upward of 6 million people. Another 3 million middle-class people lived in Asia, and 1.5 million in North America. In Europe and Asia, the numbers in the middle class reflected the regions' comparatively large populations. North America had fewer absolute numbers in the middle class, but it was the region with the largest share of its population in the middle class. In the "New World," mineral riches and plentiful and cheap agricultural land promoted trade and wealth. The Middle East benefited from its position as the crossroads of the world, connecting Europe and Asia.

It was not until 1975, almost a century and a half after the start of Queen Victoria's reign, that the number of people in the global middle class topped one billion. Two-thirds of them lived in Europe and North America. The story of the first billion people in the middle class, then, is the story of economic development and growth in these two regions of the world. It is a story of the big inventions that arose based on scientific progress, engineering ingenuity, and the economic institutions that permitted business innovation to flourish. It is equally a story about how the middle class gained political power, allying themselves with workers' or aristocratic parties at different moments in time—mostly successfully but sometimes with disastrous consequences, as in the two world wars of the twentieth century. Above all, it is a story of how the dream of building middle-class societies became the dominant economic objective of industrialized countries.

Technology, the Industrial Revolution, and the Early Growth of the Middle Class

Most accounts of the history of technological innovation that fueled the Industrial Revolution start with James Watt's steam engine. Watt did not invent the steam engine, nor was he the first to build a working machine. That had been done some seventy years earlier by an English engineer, Thomas Savery, to extract water from British coal mines. Savery's design was soon turned into a more functional machine by Thomas Newcomen. Newcomen's steam engine was in use throughout the 1700s until Watt patented a new and improved design in 1769 and started to build new steam engines in 1776. These new machines were far more efficient than the Newcomen engine and could be used in many different ways. Watt devised a design to keep the steam chambers cooler. He was able to regulate the engine speed and developed more efficient rotation using gears. He advertised his machine by comparing it to the number of horses it could replace (the old technology for removing water from mines made use of horses hauling buckets of water over a pulley system), and in doing this he introduced the term "horsepower" into the modern vernacular. Horsepower is still the most widely used measure of power in the world, although the European Union, in good bureaucratic fashion, declared in 2010 that it should be used only as a secondary measure—the principal measure being the watt.

The steam engine has been heralded as an invention that changed the world,[1] a general-purpose technology that could be adapted for many uses. It allowed mines to be dug deeper without risk of flooding. It powered new factories. It made it much easier to move from one place to another. By 1787, the American inventor John Fitch had built a steamboat to sail the Delaware River. Subsequent boats would open up the western and southern United States. In 1804, Richard Trevithick built a working prototype of the steam locomotive, giving a further push to the mobility of people and goods.

Newcomen, Watt, and Trevithick shared three traits. They connected markets by radically reducing the cost of transportation. They relied on patents for legal protection of their inventions, an important step in procuring financial support to invest in prototypes and the start of production. And they came from middling sorts of families: Newcomen's father was a merchant, Watt's a shipowner and shipwright, and Trevithick's a mining captain.

Being born into the middle class was a decisive advantage. It gave all three men the opportunity to gain the scientific knowledge needed to make technical advances and the flexibility to innovate in their own spare time. It provided them with access to financing and encouraged them to build businesses based on their inventions. In earlier times, new inventions were kept secret as a way of protecting livelihoods; the first patents were issued by the Venetian doge to glassblowers in the fifteenth century but deliberately were kept vague and often were delayed for decades to avoid copycatting. But by the mid-eighteenth century, new technologies made more money for their inventors when more people used those technologies. So inventions were popularized quickly and patented, spurring fresh innovations. In fact, Trevithick's work on high-pressure steam machines was driven by his determination to avoid paying his competitor, Watt, for using Watt's machines and patents at the Ding Dong Mine where Trevithick worked as an engineer.

Steam engines could connect factories to markets more cheaply and quickly. This allowed a shift from hand production to machine production, the essential characteristic of the Industrial Revolution. It is not coincidental that the first great general-purpose technologies were all related to transport—locomotives and steamships, carrying freight and passengers. These technologies were invented in the United Kingdom and United States but primarily adopted first in the United States. Next was the telegraph, invented in the 1830s by two Englishmen, Cooke and Wheatstone, but made more efficient and commercialized by an American, Samuel Morse of Morse code fame and, incidentally, a fine artist as well.

Later inventions also would improve connectivity: the telephone (1876), automobiles (1885), trucks (1885), cargo planes (1910), and passenger planes (1914). Ten of the fourteen most important innovations driving growth in the nineteenth century related to connectivity, according to the economists Diego Comin and Marti Mestieri, who authored a comprehensive study of the links between technology and economic growth.[2]

Once communication and connectivity were established, markets could flourish. Adam Smith already had theorized that specialization and the division of labor could drive economic progress as market size grew. More efficient factories could also become larger and achieve economies of scale. What was needed to link factories and markets in practice was the ability to transport goods and information from one place to another. As soon as that was feasible, production could happen in one place and consumption in another.

By the time of the second Industrial Revolution, new technologies including steel (1855), petroleum (1859), electricity (1882), and tractors (1892) permitted factories and farms to begin to mass produce consumer goods. This set in motion a cycle of scaled-up production with specialized jobs, leading to wealth creation, to a middle class, to innovation, and back to more efficient and larger factories.

New business processes also helped. The Joint Stock Companies Act of 1856 introduced the idea of a limited liability company (LLC)—one in which shareholders were no longer liable for a company's debts beyond their initial investments. The impact on the efficiency of how capital was allocated was massive. In the absence of limited liability, a creditor could seek repayment from a shareholder on any loans made to a company. Thus, loans would go to companies supported by the most creditworthy shareholders, not to companies with the best business ideas or innovations. Unlimited liability also locked up investors' capital. They could only sell shares to a new shareholder with equal or better creditworthiness. With the introduction of limited liability shareholding, all the information relevant for corporate finance was in a company's books—its revenues, debts, and assets, including patents. The finances of the shareholders did not matter. The law set out clear priorities for who would get paid if a company's assets had to be liquidated in the event of bankruptcy; shareholders' claims came after bankers and other lenders had been repaid in full. The limited liability company allowed middle-class entrepreneurs to start and grow a company based on its business potential rather than their own personal creditworthiness.

Technology, market connectivity, and business processes set in motion the first and second Industrial Revolutions. The share of industry in Britain's gross domestic product rose sharply in the early nineteenth century, from 23 percent in 1801 to 34 percent in 1840 and 40 percent by the end of the century, as factories took the place of artisans and craftspeople. Businesses expanded fast, using bank loans for capital to invest in new, highly productive machinery and technologies. Clerks, lawyers, bankers, and traders had to record these loans, manage contracts and invoices, settle patent claims, and transport goods from factories to towns. Railways and post offices grew to serve industry needs. Teachers in grammar schools were needed to ensure the workforce had basic reading, writing, and arithmetic skills. Nurses and doctors kept workers healthy. The whole structure of the economic system in the nineteenth and early twentieth centuries was transformed in a way that created a middle class.

Jobs, Skills, and Stable Incomes Enable the Middle Class

All these occupations called for a new category of worker: the men (and the very few women who worked outside the home at the time) who were paid a regular salary, unlike peasants or day laborers whose incomes were unpredictable. The numbers of salaried workers—a novel concept that took off during the Industrial Revolution—skyrocketed. In England in 1851, there were an estimated 44,000 clerks, accountants, and bankers; twenty years later, there were 119,000. With an average family size of over five, household heads with these occupations easily could have accounted for one-sixth of the estimated four million middle-class people in the United Kingdom in 1870.

At the same time that private-sector jobs were being created, government jobs were also expanded, although on a much smaller scale. European nations established colonies overseas to open up markets and to procure the raw materials needed for manufacturing. The Europeans needed civil servants to administer these colonies and standing armies to keep them under control. Around 1850, there were about sixteen thousand civil servants in the United Kingdom in a structure that steadily would become more meritocratic and professional over time.[3] (Until the mid-1800s, according to one historian, the government administration was neither civil nor a service, but the worst type of bureaucracy—incompetent, rent seeking, and designed to reward political favorites. There was no room for middle-class expansion there.)[4]

The salaried class comprised a different type of worker than had previously existed. People on a salary had to be technically competent and able to understand and apply a set of fixed rules. For the most part, they had to apply these rules to other specific workers to change or manage their conduct and behavior to accord with the objectives of the business or the government. Knowing how to interact with other people was quite a different skill compared to manual labor. It also differed from artisanship and self-employment. Over time, salaried workers have come to dominate the middle class, and this trend started to take hold in the mid-nineteenth century.[5]

To produce this cadre of salaried professionals, governments in the nineteenth century paid a lot of attention to improving schools and health care—what is called "human capital" by today's economists. Human capital was an important driver of the middle class, but only one factor. Without accompanying innovations in technologies and business processes, human capital could not be fully commercialized.

Although many people could read and write their own name in the early 1800s in England, there was no formal education. Only a few religious schools provided education. These were called Sunday schools because children worked the other six days. The curriculum was the Bible. A handful of schools were not affiliated with the church but were supported by philanthropy, often from the royal court. Because boys of any religion could attend, they became known as public schools—organizations that still are the foundation of the education system of the British upper and middle classes today. It was not until the Sandon Act in 1876 that parents were legally obligated to ensure that their children were educated. The 1891 Elementary Education Act provided for the state payment of school fees up to 10 shillings per head, making primary education effectively free. The Elementary Education (School Attendance) Act of 1893 raised the school-leaving age to eleven; other acts further raised it to twelve in 1899, and later to thirteen.[6]

Surprisingly, England was not at the forefront of the education wave that accompanied the Industrial Revolution. In the United States, the idea of a taxpayer-funded, formal education system had been debated since independence, with Thomas Jefferson as the champion. In a movement toward statewide public education, the idea was taken up again in the 1830s by Horace Mann, a Massachusetts state legislator who rose from humble beginnings to graduate from Brown University and who became a champion for social reforms, including public education. By 1867, the US government had established the federal Department of Education.[7]

In Europe, too, other countries had taken steps to promote education well before Britain. Prior to 1850, Belgium, Germany, Greece, Italy, Spain, and Sweden all had comprehensive national legislation that covered preprimary, primary, secondary, and, in some cases, tertiary education. In fact, it was a German educator, Friedrich Frobel, who opened the world's first kindergarten in 1837, giving a name to preschool that endures to this day and foreshadowing the movement toward early childhood education that is now viewed as the most important part of a child's learning.[8]

There was also an improvement in health throughout Europe and North America. Around 1800, one in every three children died before the age of five in these "advanced" countries, of which half died before they turned one year old.[9] In poor countries like India, closer to one out of every two children died before their fifth birthday during that time. Starting in Britain, closely followed by Belgium, France, the United States, Sweden, and Germany, health conditions steadily improved, and mortality rates decreased at a rate of about 2 percentage points every decade. (For context, the highest mortality rate today is one in eight children dying before the age of five in Somalia, whereas the average mortality rate is one in every thirteen children dying before age five in sub-Saharan Africa and one in every thirty-three children globally.)

The result of higher incomes, more education, and better health care was an explosion of the global population for the first time ever. For millennia, from 10,000 BC to 1700 AD, world population growth averaged only 0.04 percent per year. Then it started to accelerate. Around 1820, the global population was more than one billion, of which 250 million were in Europe and North America. By 1920, the world population had almost doubled to 1.91 billion, implying an average growth rate of 0.6 percent per year over the preceding century. However, 630 million people now lived in Europe and North America; the population in these places had grown at about 1 percent each year for a century, some twenty-five times faster than the long-run historical average before 1700.[10]

High population growth rates meant more people to buy manufactured goods and more houses to build. People started to move to cities, where new job opportunities emerged. Having people together in a single location turned out to be good for making markets work better. Information flowed faster; technology diffused more rapidly across businesses; and there was more competition for labor and a larger supply of willing workers. Cities developed fast, and the new technologies of electrification and lighting, water and sanitation, and personal communication and the telephone could all be introduced more rapidly there. In the United States, for example, less than 10 percent of the population lived in an urban area (defined as a place with more than 2,500 people) in 1830, but by 1930 that share had grown almost sixfold, to just under 60 percent.[11] In England and Wales, as well as Germany, urban populations grew approximately 1,000 percent over the nineteenth century, roughly 7 percent per year, although this growth was substantially slower in France, Spain, and Italy.[12]

By the end of the nineteenth century, London, New York City, Paris, and Berlin were the largest cities in the world, driven by the Industrial Revolution and driving the revolution in turn.[13] They were the centers of middle-class life.

Urbanization, population growth, health and education, and salaried jobs all boosted the level of household spending and, at the same time, encouraged spending on a new range of goods and services, which in turn created economic growth.

It is hard to imagine today, but in the early nineteenth century, most households bought very little from shops or markets. This was largely because households had to manage considerable fluctuations in income. Laborers got paid by the day when they found work; traders received unpredictable rewards depending on prices in the markets where they bought and sold; craftsmen were paid per piece by landed gentry; and agricultural workers' employment and pay depended on the harvest and the weather.

Without stable incomes, households largely spent on food and necessities (which included an average of half a liter of beer per day in England for an adult male with a middling-sized level of consumption and multiple times more in Germany).[14] They owned tables, cooking pots, and perhaps some pewter dishes but indulged in only a few luxuries and novelties: some tropical foodstuffs (tea, sugar, coffee, chocolate) and perhaps a few manufactured goods (cotton textiles, silk, porcelain, books, furniture, clocks, glassware, crockery, and metal products).[15]

But during the course of the nineteenth century, the English middle class started to consume a never-ending supply of novelties from the country's factories and workshops: fabrics for ladies' clothing in the latest new colors (such as mauve), new toys for their children, fine cutlery from Sheffield, silverware from factories like J. W. Evans in Birmingham, dinner and tea services from the Staffordshire Potteries, and plate glass from Liverpool. These were some of the novelties later displayed at Harrods and Le Bon Marché.[16]

By 1900, there were many diversions and entertainments. Theaters, music halls, libraries, museums, and art galleries were built in every major town and many minor ones, often founded by a new breed of philanthropist, successful business leaders seeking to make their hometowns more attractive places to live. Seaside towns were no longer the domain of the rich only, and places like Great Yarmouth and Blackpool developed as popular resorts for the middle and working classes.[17]

This combination of new goods being sold to new consumers earning income in new salaried occupations became the staple cycle of the middle-class economy, a cycle that in many ways still holds true today. It is one of the most powerful economic cycles that has ever formed, and its impact was profound. Around 1820, the middle class in Europe and North America might have numbered about 4.7 million people—2 percent of the population. By 1914, at the start of World War I, the middle class in Europe and North America probably numbered close to 100 million people—16 percent of the population.

From the Middling Sort to a Middle Class: Political Power in the Nineteenth Century

Members of the middle class started to exert their political power to advance their interests in the nineteenth century, but they became a dominant political force only after World War I. Without political clout, it is unlikely that the middle class could have expanded as rapidly as it did. Starting in Great Britain and spreading to America and the European continent, the middle class transformed the politics of their countries in fundamental ways. They championed an expansion of the franchise, extending votes to many more people and ultimately creating a critical mass of politically active middle-class people. And they fought, at least initially, for economic principles of protection of private property, small government with limited taxes, free trade, and limited regulation. By allying themselves with moral causes—opposing slavery and child labor, for example—the middle class in various countries became associated broadly with a general love for liberty and freedom.

Thus, the middle class became the backbone of what is today called liberal democracy. As the American political scientist Francis Fukuyama would write many years later, "Over time, however, the liberal and the democratic agendas began to converge, and democracy became a middle-class goal. Rule of law and democratic accountability are, after all, alternative means of constraining power, and in practice are often mutually supportive." He went on to argue:

> The key insight is that democracy is desired most strongly by one specific social group in society: the middle class. If we are to understand the likelihood of democracy emerging, we need to evaluate the strength of the middle class relative to other social groups that prefer other forms of government, such as the old, landed oligarchy who are inclined to support authoritarian systems, or radicalized groups of peasants or urban poor who are focused on economic redistribution.[18]

Fukuyama was challenging the Marxist view that "the lower middle-class has no special class interests."[19] Marx believed that only the great capitalist class and the proletariat were capable of governing society and that the middle class was simply a disparate, but potentially numerically large, group of shopkeepers, artisans, and others who could be useful allies at times (when the proletariat party was in opposition) but who should be treated with caution when the middle-class party interests were in coalitions with governments in power. Ultimately, Marx believed that the middle-class support for private property, credit, and other features of liberal economics would be a permanent barrier to true socialism. In this, he was probably right. The middle class has rejected socialism and collective property rights while fighting for individual freedoms and has recruited most of the working class to its way of thinking.

The growth of the middle class's political power does not mean that they had their own political party or were always linked with any of the traditional parties. The middle class could not be pinned down as leaning toward conservatives, progressives, nationalists, or any other label. To the contrary, middle-class politics has taken on many identities during different times and in different places. These twists and turns have had one thing in common: each time, the middle class emerged as a stronger political force.

Growth of Middle-Class Political Power in Great Britain

In Great Britain, the origins of the middle class as a politically powerful group can be traced to the early nineteenth century. William Pitt the Younger, the prime minister of Great Britain, had introduced a progressive income tax in 1799 to pay for military expenditures linked to the French revolutionary wars and the Napoleonic Wars. The tax was deeply unpopular to the extent that even military victories could not be celebrated. "Why rejoice," wrote one commentator in the *Monthly Repository* in 1809, in the middle of the Napoleonic Wars, "while the burden of taxation presses so heavily on the middle classes of society, so as to leave the best part of the community little to hope and everything to fear?"[20] This is one of the earliest records of a comment about the middling sort as a political class. It also foretells one of the earliest political successes of the middle class. The income tax was repealed in 1815, based on an alliance between the middle class and the upper class, who similarly pushed for its abolishment.

At least some historians believe that Victorian Britain represented a "triumph of the middle class."[21] The English historian, politician, and writer Thomas Babington Macaulay was one of the most eloquent proponents of the view that the social and economic changes wrought by the Industrial Revolution also had to be accompanied by political change that would advance economic growth. Macaulay espoused free trade and movement of people, abolishment of slavery, allowing women to own property, and freedom of the press. His accounts of history were stories about how people strove to be free and to pursue the opportunities to prosper that science and industry offered. He became so famous that one commentator later claimed the three essential works of civilization were the Bible, Shakespeare, and Macaulay.[22]

Macaulay chronicled and advocated for some of the sweeping changes in the Victorian political landscape. Although Britain had a parliamentary system in the 1830s, few people were allowed to vote—only around 3 percent of the total population. The electoral system divided the country into constituencies of boroughs (towns), counties, and universities, each of which could send members to Parliament. The 1832

Reform Act updated the boundaries of these constituencies to reflect in small part the rapid urbanization and population growth taking place. Nevertheless, only people living in certain properties could vote, so most of the population was completely disenfranchised.

In truth, Britain in the early 1800s was run by its rural gentry. About one-fifth of Parliament's seats were reserved for places with fewer than fifty voters, a system that was easily exploited by prominent families. The problem with these "rotten boroughs," as they came to be called, was so bad that in 1831 there were riots against the system across the country.

The Reform Act was a first response to this civil disorder, giving more people the right to vote, offering more seats to the industrialized areas of northern England and to urban areas relative to rural areas. The Tories, the conservative party of the time, were overwhelmingly opposed to the bill. Thanks to their domination in the House of Lords, they were able to derail the first two attempts to pass the bill, but overwhelming popular demand created the needed support for the liberal Whig parties to finally carry the day.

The Reform Act was a huge victory for the members of the middle class, but it was achieved through an alliance with workers and trade unions rather than with the landed gentry, who were the middle class's partner in abolishing the income tax. After the Reform Act, the middle class primarily voted for the Whigs and later for the Liberal Party, despite the fact that these parties were still largely led by and dominated by the old aristocrats; just look at the names of the prime ministers elected with middle-class support: the second Earl Grey, the second Viscount Melbourne, and the third Viscount Palmerston. Even William Ewert Gladstone, thrice-appointed prime minister for the Liberals, was the son of one of the largest slave owners in the British Empire and was initially a Conservative—hardly a traditional middle-class champion.

The Whigs were free traders, influenced by the writings of Adam Smith. This earned them the support of the middle class. The middle class had become particularly opposed to tariffs that Britain had imposed on imports of wheat from the continent. They wanted the tariffs repealed to drive down the price of food, which would allow manufacturers to pay lower wages and become more competitive, but this was resisted by the politically powerful rural gentry of the time, who made considerable profits on the grain they produced at home.

Thus was born the Anti-Corn Law League, the first openly middle-class pressure group. (Confusingly, corn referred to all cereal grains, including wheat, oats, and barley in England at that time.) Led by Richard Cobden, a self-made industrialist from northern England, the league was deliberately organized around a single issue to generate maximum support. It had one clear message: repeal the tariff on "corn." The Anti-Corn Law League fought through elections to raise its representation in Parliament, with some modest success thanks to the Reform Act. But the league's real power came from organizing mass rallies and protests backed by moral and economic arguments that were easy to understand and that inspired great passion among the masses, who wanted cheaper food.

In 1846, the Corn Laws were repealed through a coalition between the sitting Tory prime minister, Robert Peel, and the Whig opposition. Peel's support was pragmatic—he and fellow Tories worried that, without some change, a far more revolutionary upheaval could occur. The Whigs' support was ideological—they believed in markets free from government interference.

Cobden's success led him to openly and more broadly challenge Peel to drop his Tory traditions and take up the mantle of representing the middle class. In a famous letter to the prime minister, Cobden asked, "Do you shrink from the post of governing through the bona fide representatives of the middle class? Look at the facts, and can the country be otherwise ruled at all? . . . Some man must of necessity rule the state through its governing class. The Reform Bill decreed it: the passing of the Corn Bill has realised it."[23] In his reply, Peel studiously ignored mentioning the middle class. He was, after all, a baronet and a staunch believer in monarchy and the rule of law. To this day, police officers in Britain are nicknamed "bobbies" in recognition of Peel's role in establishing the London Metropolitan Police Force. Peel was not going to acknowledge the legitimacy of a new class that would challenge the existing order.

And so the process of shifting coalitions to address middle-class issues continued throughout the nineteenth century. The middle class lent their political weight to pressure the various governments of the day to enact reforms on very specific issues that would advance their interests. In addition to the Great Reform Act of 1832 and the repeal of the Corn Laws in 1846, other bills on urbanization, connectivity, and education—the middle-class catalysts identified earlier—also helped the middle class to grow and prosper and were passed due to support of the middle class. A slew of reforms demonstrated the political power of the middle class, allying them either with workers or with the upper class.

The Municipal Corporations Act (1835) established a system of elected town councils to manage local affairs after a finding by a royal commission that the existing corporations "neither possess nor deserve the confidence or respect of Your Majesty's subjects."[24] The new boroughs were mandated to set up police forces and to publish audited financial accounts each year. The act was extended in 1882 to permit more direct control over urban development through the purchase of land and construction of municipal buildings.

The Railway Acts in 1844 and 1846 provided regulations designed to permit cheap rail travel. The railways had in-built class distinctions, with their first-, second-, and third-class carriages, but the 1844 act required third-class carriages on every train to have a maximum fare per mile. They also had to have covered seats. The 1846 act weighed in on the great gauge wars between companies using broad-gauge tracks and those using narrow gauges, standardizing the narrow-gauge version over time. Intense competition among the "big four" private operators of the time meant that passenger transport grew rapidly—from negligible levels in 1840 to one billion passenger rail trips around 1900.

The Elementary Education Act in 1870 gave local authorities greater power over schools in their districts. Although nominally concerned with improving the education and productivity of the labor force, especially after the second Great Reform Act in 1867 had doubled the voting population from one million to two million (still men only), the Elementary Education Act in Great Britain gained support among conservatives who witnessed the tactical advantage an educated army gave Prussia in its war against Austria in 1866. This education act was followed in quick succession by an 1876 act prohibiting children from working on farms until they were older than eleven years of age and had achieved minimum academic standards, an 1880 act mandating school attendance, and an 1891 act making elementary education free.

Later, facing trade union mobilization and electoral threats from the newly formed Labour Party, the governing Liberals in Britain established worker pensions, unemployment, and health insurance between 1906 and 1911, incorporating elements that would ultimately prove very valuable to the middle class.

Growth of Middle-Class Political Power in the United States

Great Britain was not alone in finding the middle class to be a potent political force. The same experience was taking place in the United States.

The United States started the nineteenth century with the distinct advantage of not having an established aristocracy. True, it had an upper class of very rich men, but they gained their status through business rather than through divine right. Until the mid-nineteenth century, the United States was a two-class land of wealthy urban elites and manual laborers, with only a few artisans. But as economic growth took hold, American jobs were created in occupations that did not require manual labor. Small retailers, small entrepreneurs, and skilled artisans initially, and then, as these were squeezed out by large corporations and manufacturers, clerks and white-collar wage earners became the cornerstone of the middle class.

Unlike in Europe, class was not the defining characteristic of how American society was organized or of the struggles it faced during the nineteenth century. More obvious cleavages in society included race and the legacy of slavery, ethnic distinctions as serial waves of immigrants came to the country from abroad, and religious divisions, especially between Catholics and Protestants. The depth of these and other issues was most readily seen in the different values between the South and the North.

Nevertheless, class did play an important role in US politics. More than anything else, the American middle class developed a unique culture of stability, freedom, self-discipline, moderation, and independence. It was a culture not just of individual advancement, but of how society should be organized. It led to the temperance movement and volunteerism, especially among middle-class women, which would shape their political views. Most importantly, a concept of behavior and lifestyle developed around patterns of consumption. The American middle class started to define itself in terms of consumerism rather than in terms of occupation.

By the 1870s, chain stores like A&P and Woolworth's had opened, orienting themselves specifically toward the middle classes in suburban areas, in contrast with fashionable department stores such as Macy's or Gimbels, which catered to the wealthy. New building technologies permitted stores to have large glass windows, countertops, and display cases so that goods could be seen. By the end of the century, L. Frank Baum, of *Wizard of Oz* fame, had founded the National Association of Window Trimmers and began publishing *The Store Window* journal to advise businesses on space usage and promotion.[25]

Other iconic companies, like Sears, Roebuck and Company and Montgomery Ward, had a different strategy, offering mail-order sales at transparent, low prices. With retailers competing to sell goods and with banks offering credit, the range of goods on offer expanded. By 1895, the Sears catalog was more than five hundred pages and included sewing machines, bicycles, sporting goods, dolls, stoves, and even groceries and automobiles, earning it the moniker "the consumer bible." All forms of dry goods, consumer durables, hardware, and furniture could be bought by catalog and on credit. And the choices made defined one's class. As Roland Marchand described in his "Parable of the Democracy of Goods,"[26] in an era when access to products became more important than access to the means of production, Americans quickly accepted the notion that a better lifestyle meant purchasing the right clothes, the best hair cream, and the shiniest shoes.

Politics was a major threat to this lifestyle. Corruption and waste in government was rampant during the Gilded Age of the late nineteenth century, especially in cities. Left to themselves, local governments could tax the middle class and make life intolerable in the urban and suburban areas where the middle class lived. So the middle classes pushed to put more control in the hands of citizens and to make local politics more accountable to themselves. They fought for direct initiatives, referenda, and recalls, first enshrined into the state constitution of Oregon in the early twentieth century and from there expanded to several other western states. They pushed for prohibition because saloons were where much of the corrupt vote buying took place. They enacted voter registration lists to prevent multiple voting. They pushed for female enfranchisement.

Yet the middle class was not altogether democratic in the modern sense of the word. They wanted their own kind of people (white Protestant Anglo-Saxons) to vote, but not others. Literacy tests kept out manual laborers. Southern states used a range of procedures to effectively disenfranchise Black voters in a backlash to the Fifteenth Amendment, which had given Black citizens the vote after the Civil War. The same tactics were used in other states to limit the influence of the immigrants who were arriving by the millions each year around the turn of the century.

Although expanding rapidly, the American middle class was too small itself to have a leading voice in politics. They fell between the moneyed upper class, who were wealthy enough to buy enough votes and influence, and the massive numbers of working-class voters who were organizing themselves into the Socialist Party of America (SPA), founded in 1901, and the Industrial Workers of the World (IWW), founded in 1905. To gain support from workers, the middle class took on many prolabor causes, such as education, child labor laws, trust busting, and regulation.

Education reform fit naturally with the middle-class culture and lifestyle. It provided the basis of individualism and the freedom of each family to improve their own condition. It lent itself to modernization and professionalism. The impact of school and curricula reform could be measured through written standardized testing, a system that steadily replaced oral testing in the mid-nineteenth century. American education movements were grassroots, led by each community, very much in line with the middle-class focus on local improvements, and reliant on associations rather than individualism as the driver of social change. In 1900, the College Entrance Examination Board was established to introduce a system of college admission that was more meritocratic rather than relying on personal recommendations from important people. College became an early ladder for the American middle class.

The combination of these two causes—rooting out government corruption and advancing opportunities through education for all—was at the heart of the progressive political movement. The progressives achieved direct election of senators through the Seventeenth Amendment, prohibition in the Eighteenth Amendment, and women's suffrage in the Nineteenth Amendment. The height of progressive political power came at the very beginning of the twentieth century, when Theodore Roosevelt served as president from 1901 to 1909. Famous for trust busting and for environmentalism, President Roosevelt championed the idea of government in the service of the (voting) people. Many of his reforms, including establishing the presidency as a strong, efficient, and impactful executive body, remain central to American political life.

Growth of Middle-Class Political Power in Europe

In continental Europe, politics was also being shaped by shifting alliances between the middle class and either workers or elites. In Scandinavian countries, a "red-green alliance" of urban workers and prosperous rural farmers successfully pushed for a pension law extending benefits to all citizens. As industrialization and urbanization proceeded, white-collar professionals formed a "red-white alliance" and gradually replaced farmers as political power players in the alliance. Because the middle class valued stability, this alliance worked to advance social protections that not only reduced poverty and vulnerability by limiting people's exposure to risk, but also helped to tamp down radicalization and social upheaval among the industrial workforce and its accompanying political movements—socialist parties and revolutionary communes. Countering the threat of socialism was paramount in the decision of Otto von Bismarck's government in Germany to enact three basic components of social protections between 1883 and 1889, with middle-class support: health care, accident insurance, and unemployment and old-age pensions. Similarly, France established free medical assistance and support programs for the elderly in the 1890s.

Without political power augmented through serial expansion of voting rights, the middle class surely would not have been able to expand as rapidly as it did across the industrializing world. Seemingly small differences in how this power was used in the nineteenth century, however, have resulted in profound differences in the nature of the middle class to this day. Systems of majoritarian voting practiced in Anglo-Saxon countries, where representatives in parliament or its equivalent are selected based on winning a majority (or plurality) of votes from their districts, have mostly led to two-party competitions in which the middle class typically allies itself with conservative upper-class forces to keep taxation low. On the other hand, systems of proportional representation as practiced by most Scandinavian countries, in which a party's number of seats is linked to its share of the vote (often using rather complex formulas), have tended to support multiparty coalitions in which the middle class allies itself with center-left movements to extract as many social protections as possible from the system.

In both systems, the middle class has found a way to benefit regardless of the rules under which democracy is actually practiced. This is a claim that neither the upper class nor the working class can make: they become winners or losers in different democratic systems, constantly competing for an alliance with the middle class.

An Illiberal Turn for the Middle Class

By and large, middle-class politics has advanced broad-based prosperity. But the middle class has also been deluded into throwing their support behind nationalist forces, leading to two world wars and the largest economic depression in history.

The American progressives strove to link themselves to science, efficiency, and modernity but on occasion could be led astray by wrong-headed ideas and faulty evidence. A dark part of the progressives' legacy is the embrace of eugenics, a narrative that human society could be improved by selective breeding. Eugenics, as proposed by its originator, the English statistician Sir Francis Galton, had two pillars for improving the population's genetic stock. It encouraged policies such as forced sterilization to stop reproduction by those displaying undeserving traits (those deemed by political power brokers to be genetically inferior) and to simultaneously subsidize children in families with superior traits. Apart from the obvious violation of human rights, eugenics was based on the fallacy that genes determined social behavior. Bizarrely, Edward Ross, one of the most influential American progressive sociologists at the turn of the twentieth century, believed that Anglo-Saxons were better suited to rural life, whereas "Latins, Slavs, Asiatics and Hebrews," who were emigrating to America in large numbers, were better adapted to industrial capitalism and would therefore displace white people unless forceful government action was taken.[27] President Roosevelt subscribed to these views, asserting that "race suicide"—the outbreeding of a "superior" human lineage by a more prolific but "less desirable" lineage—was the greatest problem of civilization. These views on eugenics influenced American approaches toward immigration for decades, and echoes still reverberate today.

Eugenics was not the only massive blunder made by progressives. Recall that they were ardent free traders, both for the variety of goods that were made available by trade as well as for the expansive markets and benefits of specialization that free trade created. Across the Atlantic, all the major European countries had been busy establishing colonies to bolster their trading positions. African colonies provided raw materials, and Asian colonies provided large markets as well as military outposts from which force could be projected. The British settled in Shanghai in 1843 after the first Opium War, when they forced the Chinese to permit the import and sale of opium grown in Bengal, claiming that the principle of free trade was more important than the public health issues of opium addiction. After the second Opium War, other countries, including the United States, France, and Russia, also received trade privileges in China that were extracted through force.

President Teddy Roosevelt was a strong believer in the idea that a more muscular foreign policy would be in the national interest of America. He replaced the relative isolationism of previous governments with a forceful consolidation and extension of the gains made after the Spanish-American War of 1898. His motto "speak softly and carry a big stick" was deftly used to persuade Panama to permit construction of a canal that, when completed in 1914, shortened the sea route from San Francisco to New York by eight thousand miles. The desire to trade more and to reduce the cost of trade again proved decisive in driving foreign policy and military adventurism. In the early twentieth century, US administrations would dispatch troops on a dozen different occasions to Mexico and the Caribbean to "seize customs houses, reorganize finances, or attempt to control the outcome of an internal revolution," according to historian Daniel T. Rodgers.[28]

Widespread acceptance of the idea that countries could and should use force to gain trade and economic advantage allowed many of the forces of nationalism, imperialism, and militarism to gain strength. Nationalism—the idea of promoting the interests of one's own country and proffering allegiance to the country rather than to a divinely appointed monarch—was particularly popular among middle-class intellectuals and professionals. Of course, nationalism was not purely a middle-class phenomenon—all classes displayed elements of it—but the middle class provided the intellectual underpinnings of the movement.

Nationalist sentiment exploded in Europe with the assassination of the Archduke Franz Ferdinand by Gavrilo Princip, a Bosnian Serb born into a peasant family and a member of the terrorist Black Hand Society. The Slavs in the Balkans had thrown off the rule of the Ottoman Empire some years earlier but then watched Austria assert control over Bosnia. The nationalists were determined to respond. After three prior failed bombing efforts, the assassins seized their opportunity when the archduke and his wife were driven through Sarajevo, the capital city of the annexed region of Bosnia and Herzegovina. At first the assassination was treated as an internal matter to be resolved within the Austro-Hungarian Empire. But the authorities held neighboring Serbia responsible for sponsoring the Black Hand and declared war on the weaker country when the conditions set forth by Austria in an ultimatum were not accepted. Serbia had an alliance with Russia, which in turn was allied with Britain and France in the Triple Entente, so these major powers were dragged into the fight. When Austria's ally, Germany, honored its own Triple Alliance and entered the fray, all the major European countries (except Italy, which initially remained neutral) descended into war and chaos. The unthinkable and unexpected would come to pass because of a series of errors and miscalculations.

It would be a stretch to say that World War I was caused by the expansion of the middle class and the competition among its members. But the forces of industrialization, modernization, technological and scientific knowledge, trade, and foreign adventurism that lay behind the growth of the middle class were the same forces that led to the war. All the major economies except Austria-Hungary had built up a war chest of gold reserves in the decade preceding the war. They had enjoyed strong economic growth, partly fueled by public spending on the military, especially the navy in the cases of Germany and Britain. Germany's gross domestic product (GDP) had surpassed that of Britain, and its pig iron output was almost double that of Britain by 1913. There was every expectation that the war would be short (maybe six months). Kaiser Wilhelm II (Queen Victoria's grandson) promised his troops that they would be home before the autumn leaves fell. There was a consensus that the conflict should not be accompanied by economic warfare or blockades. It looked like it would not be too costly for the middle class.

Like so many other assumptions about World War I, the idea that it would be short and relatively inexpensive was massively wrong. The war was enormously consequential. There were around forty million casualties, military and civilian, roughly divided equally between the dead and wounded. At the time, the total population of Europe, which saw the bulk of the fighting and the casualties, only amounted to slightly more than five hundred million. Military casualties on their own exceeded 10 percent of the population in France and Germany, and more than 5 percent of the British population.

In both Entente and Alliance armies, there were large casualties among officers. Officers were drawn primarily from the aristocratic upper class, a tradition dating back to the nineteenth century, when it was still common for officers to buy their commissions in the British army. The more senior the position, the more they had to pay. This was how the infamous Lord Cardigan (James Thomas Brudenell), the general who in 1854 disastrously ordered the charge of the Light Brigade, pitting cavalry against Russian cannons in the Crimean War, got his appointment—money, not merit. So officers had to be rich and were therefore drawn from the rich and upper middle classes. Their reward was social standing accentuated by ornate uniforms and conspicuous gold tassels. An officer had to be a gentleman, and most gentlemen aspired to be officers.

The system of purchasing military commissions had been abolished in Britain in 1870 and replaced by a system of choosing officers from among the graduates of a special school, the Royal Military Academy at Sandhurst. Although technically a radical reform, in practice the impact on the class background of officers was negligible. Only the rich could afford the tuition fees, uniforms, and equipment required to attend Sandhurst.

During World War I, this tradition of the wealthy being the officer class was destroyed. Casualties among officers were so high and the expansion of the army was so large that there were simply not enough aristocrats to fill all the positions. Officers had to be recruited from the rank and file. But to ensure that this did not change their class position, these officers were bestowed the honorific title of "temporary gentlemen."[29] The idea was that once the war was over, the status normally given to a ranking military officer would be withdrawn and the demobilized officer would return to his lower-class position. Not surprisingly, this was not a popular move, and it pushed the middle class to ally themselves more closely with the working class in the post–World War I period and to emerge stronger in their fights against the upper class.

Across the Atlantic, middle-class progressives, still led by Teddy Roosevelt even though he was no longer president, were keen to enter the war. In addition to historical ties with Britain and France, Americans were concerned about the impact the war was having on trade. The British and French were using their navies to prevent goods from reaching Germany and Austria. So the United States had to use intermediaries, in Sweden and other Scandinavian countries, to continue to trade. The progressives wanted to end the war swiftly by throwing their weight behind the Entente. Roosevelt asked President Woodrow Wilson for permission to raise a division of the Rough Riders, the cavalry regiment that Roosevelt cofounded, which had been so successful during the Spanish-American War. Wilson was skeptical and initially turned Roosevelt down. World War I was a different challenge—a war of primitive tanks, machine guns, and poison gases, not one that would be won through the kind of heroic cavalry charge that Roosevelt was suggesting.

America did enter the war but deliberately and at its own pace. In 1915, the Germans sank the *Lusitania*, a British ship carrying passengers and cargo, at a cost of more than a thousand lives, including over one hundred Americans. This generated widespread animosity. The Germans then resorted to an all-out submarine blockade of Entente countries in 1917, targeting all ships, including those of neutral nations like the United States. It was perhaps the straw that broke the camel's back. Within a year of the American entry to support the Entente in 1917, the war was over.

There is little doubt that, in a cruel way, World War I had the effect of creating a power vacuum in Europe and a shake-up of class alliances. The war decimated the upper-class gentry across Europe. It also severely indebted all the countries involved and shifted power to the creditors, principally in the United States. With the opening of the American Midwest, grain prices fell in Europe in the late nineteenth and early twentieth centuries, hurting the finances of the aristocracy, who still earned significant rents on their vast holdings of rural land, although many had also diversified into industry and banking.

Military victory in the "Great War" temporarily boosted the power of the old aristocracy in the Entente countries, but they were nevertheless severely weakened, and their countries were heavily indebted. But it was not the physical or economic catastrophe that had the greatest impact. Rather, it was the seeding of an idea that government, through its ability to control, administer, and expand into areas of its choosing, could drive the fortunes of countries and their citizens. The early liberal principle of small government died in the trenches of the Great War.

The middle class, too, suffered. Before the war, there had been an emerging international middle-class movement in the sense of a structured organization to pay attention to middle-class interests (typically, low taxes) and to articulate a vision of a meritocratic and just middle-class society. The Association de Défense des Classes Moyennes (Association for the Defence of the Middle Classes) was founded in 1908 in Paris and held an international congress every year in various European cities.[30] But after the war and the Bolshevik Revolution, the middle class was left fearful and splintered, caught between communists and capitalists, and unable to unify the patchwork of artisans, small business owners, salaried wage earners, civil servants, and professionals who constituted the middle class. The foundation of the middle class as a group that intermediated between capitalists and workers, and hence provided stability to society, had to be reviewed in the context of crisis.[31]

For the middle class in France, the immediate post–World War I years were particularly difficult economically. The value of whatever meager savings that families may have had was destroyed by price increases. The government could, at best, fund the reconstruction of destroyed infrastructure, but no one had money for new productive investment or creation of new jobs. The French political scientist J. Artur wrote, "'I suffer, therefore I am' might now be the motto of our middle class, crushed in its dignity, its preference for saving, and its fundamental optimism by a postwar social storm that has modified traditional French society as much as the barbarian invasions."[32]

In the Alliance countries, particularly Germany, there was a vacuum of power. The old aristocracy had lost the war, and the working class was being wooed by socialist revolutionaries, buoyed by their success in forcing Czar Nicholas II to abdicate in 1917. To what could the middle class turn? The answer was first to try to construct a modern, liberal democracy, the Weimar Republic in Germany, and when that experiment failed, the middle class turned to nationalism and fascism.

Germany went through hyperinflation in 1922 and 1923 followed by a period of stabilization and rapid recovery from 1924 through 1928 (the "Golden Years of the Weimar"), but then it suffered a collapse in 1929 through 1933 as the Great Depression set in. The story is complicated, but a thumbnail sketch is that large war reparations depleted Germany's foreign exchange reserves, forcing it to print domestic money without any backing. The result was hyperinflation—anathema to the middle class—that was subsequently overcome but at the cost of massive external borrowing, mostly from American banks. When the Great Depression started after the US stock market crash of October 1929, American bankers called in their loans, and Germany entered its own depression.

The American sociologist and political scientist Seymour Martin Lipset, in a classic analysis titled *Political Man*,[33] would later write that fascism originated in the middle class, specifically in young, rural, small-town, self-employed segments of the German population—the "petty bourgeois." Added to the disaffected were a large number of civil servants (about seven hundred thousand) who were laid off during the stabilization and recovery period in an effort to cut Germany's budget deficit. Together, these groups formed a formidable voting bloc. Adolf Hitler's National Socialist German Workers' Party (NSDAP) vote share rose from 3 percent in 1928 to 43 percent in 1933.[34]

The middle class in Germany by itself was not large enough to account for most of the Nazi votes. The Nazis also gained support from the working class. But the appeal of fascism to the middle class was clear: among the twenty-five points in the national socialist program were commitments to national education, a ban on child labor, land reform and its appropriation for public policies, lower taxes, old-age pensions, and, of course, in a continuation of the eugenics tradition, racial superiority of a single group.

In these policy programs espousing traditional middle-class issues, the middle class saw a new path to progress. This was doubly attractive to young people who also saw in Nazism an action program that satisfied their psychological needs of a lust for power and revenge to offset the humiliation of earlier defeat in the war. Erich Fromm, the German social psychologist, put it this way: "Freedom, though it has brought [modern man] independence and rationality, has made him isolated and, thereby, anxious and powerless. This isolation is unbearable and the alternatives he is confronted with are either to escape from the burden of this freedom into new dependencies and submission, or to advance to the full realization of positive freedom which is based upon the uniqueness and individuality of man."[35] Those choosing to support the Nazis chose the path of submission.

In Italy, where fascism originated (the word is derived from the Italian *fasci*, meaning "bundles," or leagues of fighting groups), Benito Mussolini's program included long-standing middle-class issues including votes for women, a minimum wage, and a reorganization and modernization of the railways and transport sector.

In brief, fascists offered the middle class the very social programs they had advocated for during the nineteenth century—expanded suffrage, education, and connectivity, as well as lower taxes. But it was a deal with the devil. The fascists also used violence and thuggery to distort and control voting processes, and once in power, they used the levers of the state to ensure they remained in power.

There are historians who argue that World War II (and other smaller wars in the years preceding it) was a consequence of leaderships that desperately feared falling domestic living standards and so felt forced into military expansionism.[36] Japan's control of Manchuria in 1931 and parts of China in 1937, Mussolini's invasion of Ethiopia in 1935, and Germany's annexation of Austria and the Sudetenland in what was then Czechoslovakia in 1938 not only fueled domestic nationalism but also led to control over natural resources that were needed to offset the economic pain of the Depression.

For the global middle class, World War II was a demographic calamity. It not only halted the growth of the global middle class, but also changed its composition. In Europe, the middle class became one-third smaller. In East Asia, where the bulk of the middle class at the time was concentrated in Japan, the middle class was almost cut in half. It was only in North America that the middle class prospered and grew in numbers. As a result, almost half of the global middle class was concentrated in North America by the end of the war. In 1946, the United States alone had around 108 million people in middle-class families. The United Kingdom had the next largest concentration of middle-class families, amounting to about 29 million people or just one-quarter of the number in America. The former USSR probably had less than 3 million middle-class people after the war.

The American Dream and Social Contracts with the Middle Class

The immediate aftermath of World War II provided an opportunity to forge a new social contract between government and its citizenry. The experience of the Great Depression had exposed the perils of unfettered capitalism with small government. The socialist experiment in the Soviet Union went against the fundamental tenets that the Western middle class held dear—property rights, individual liberty, and personal responsibility. After World War II, the middle class in Europe struggled to find its own footing in much the same way they had struggled after World War I.

This time, however, was different. The concept of the middle class, which had been exported from Europe to the United States in the nineteenth century, was now about to be reexported back to Europe from America, where the middle class was alive and well.

The Making of the American Middle-Class Dream

The "American dream" of the middle class had been clearly expressed by James Truslow Adams in *The Epic of America*, written in 1931. Adams took care to clarify that he was not just talking about having a car, a house, and a good-paying job, but was expressing a far deeper concept. He dreamed of an organization of society "in which each man and each woman shall be able to attain to the fullest stature of which they are innately capable, and be recognized by others for what they are, regardless of the fortuitous circumstances of birth or position."[37]

It was this American dream that the United States encouraged in Europe, in part with the backing of money disbursed through the Marshall Plan. It was a dream of meritocracy and excellence, oriented toward achieving broad-based prosperity. It set out the ladders for success in the corporate world and for a powerful, albeit limited, government role in providing guardrails for the market economy to avoid the worst effects of the Great Depression.

In essence, the American dream was a social contract between government and citizens that would use the power of the government to promote stability, meritocracy, and opportunity for everyone. It was based on the values of hard work, saving for the future, and individual responsibility for success or failure. It was a vision of an affluent middle-class society.

The foundation of the American dream was unquestionably the provision of good jobs. By 1944, when the United States had geared up its factories to produce tanks, ships, planes, and munitions for the war effort, unemployment had fallen to just 1.2 percent, the lowest rate ever recorded either before or since. The peacetime economy had never generated so many jobs, for both men and women. As troops returned and policymakers' thoughts focused on transitioning the economy back to civilian production, the issue of ensuring adequate employment for men was paramount. For women, the situation was slightly different. About ten million women were working in the nonagricultural sector before the war, some 20 percent of the total female labor force (but only 15 percent of married women worked outside the home). During the war, six million more women entered the war economy, many in manufacturing, where they accounted for a third of the total workforce. But immediately after the war, four million left the labor force, including most of those in manufacturing. They were not unemployed but returning to lives as homemakers.

In 1946, President Harry Truman passed the Employment Act. The act was notable both for what it said and for what it did not say. It assigned to the federal government the responsibility to provide "conditions under which there will be afforded useful employment for those able, willing, and seeking work, and to promote maximum employment, production, and purchasing power."[38] This language was a careful compromise; the original draft of what was initially presented as the Full Employment Bill stated, "All Americans able to work and seeking work have the right to useful, remunerative, regular, and full-time employment, and it is the policy of the United States to assure the existence at all times of sufficient employment opportunities to enable all Americans who have finished their schooling and who do not have full-time housekeeping responsibilities to freely exercise this right."[39]

The 1946 Employment Act established the basis for a middle-class economy in America founded on consumerism and purchasing power: plentiful jobs, economic growth, and low inflation. Rather than calling for a federal commitment to full employment, the 1946 act avoided prescribing specific policy actions in favor of requiring the federal government to report on the state of the economy and jobs. This report was to be written by the newly established Council of Economic Advisers and transmitted to the Joint Economic Committee of the House and Senate, which would then make recommendations to Congress on any economic policy reforms that might be required.

The three-pronged economic strategy of jobs, growth, and price stability was perfectly designed for the middle class. Good jobs and wage growth underpinned middle-class lifestyles. Economic growth provided the opportunities for new small businesses, the traditional bastion of the middle class. And low inflation and interest rates protected their financial assets as the middle class saved for old age and for the purchase of durable goods—the houses, cars, televisions, vacuum cleaners, dishwashers, and other appliances that represented the middle-class lifestyle.

Even before the war ended, this strategy was being implemented, although not fully articulated as the basis for government policy. The GI Bill of Rights, passed in 1944, offered cheap mortgages, low-interest small business loans, unemployment compensation, and various tuition payments to veterans returning home from military service. By the time the bill ended in 1956, 7.8 million out of the 16 million returning veterans, or about one-fifth of the total nonfarm employment after the war, had taken advantage of the educational benefits in the GI Bill, contributing to a huge expansion in the education and productivity of the workforce.

The boost in productivity growth, coupled with mass consumption by the middle class, ushered in a quarter-century period stretching from the war to around 1973 that has come to be known as the golden age of American consumerism. This golden age, a reference to Mark Twain's prescient commentary of the last quarter of the nineteenth century as the Gilded Age,[40] saw productivity and hourly compensation almost double.

By the end of the golden age, nine out of ten Americans belonged to the middle class.

Exactly how this came about is still the subject of considerable debate. Some historians argue that it was because technologies developed for the war were repurposed for civilian use. Certainly, there was more automation, more efficient use of inputs (for example, oil replacing coal as a source of power), and more scientific advances. Fertilizers, pesticides, tractors, and modern seed varieties raised agricultural yields. Whole new industries emerged at scale, producing televisions, airplanes, and computers. And of course, in the immortal words of *The Graduate*, "I just want to say one word to you. . . . Plastics."[41]

Manufacturing played a prominent role. By 1969, almost nineteen million American workers were employed in manufacturing (out of ninety-one million total employed).

An alternative explanation gives more emphasis to the demand side of the economy. The head of the United Auto Workers (UAW) union at the time, Walter Reuther, argued that the war had demonstrated the main economic problem was not an inability to produce more things but to sustain the purchasing power to buy them. After all, in the five years between 1940 and 1945, the US gross national product (GNP) grew by three-quarters, with 19 percent growth in 1941 alone, thanks to demand for weapons and munitions to fight the war.[42]

Reuther's argument was that America needed more, and stronger, trade unions to ensure demand kept pace with rising productivity. In 1954, about one-third of US workers belonged to a union. Starting with an agreement between the UAW and General Motors in 1948, unions negotiated wages based on productivity and cost-of-living increases. This was a new social contract in America, a negotiation between corporate management and labor. It reflected a balance between supply-siders and those arguing for more demand management, as exemplified in this exchange between Reuther and a senior manager at Ford:

> Ford executive: "Walter, look at these automatically controlled machines. How are you going to collect union dues from them?"
>
> Reuther: "How are you going to get them to buy Fords?"[43]

During the golden age, consumption boomed even without extensive unionization. Americans had been saving during the war, partly because they were encouraged to buy government bonds to help the war effort and partly because goods were rationed and people could not spend all their money. In 1945, they saved 21 percent of their personal disposable income. So once the war was over, they had plenty of money coming in from wage earnings and from maturing war bonds. They went on a buying spree, purchasing everything from homes and all the appliances and furniture needed to fill them to cars.[44] By the end of the 1950s, three-quarters of American households owned at least one car. The golden age ushered in flush toilets, televisions, and air conditioners in millions of homes across the country, visits to Disneyland, and vacations abroad. Led by advertisers using a range of psychological techniques, Americans were persuaded that material consumption of goods and services was the ticket to the good life.

Meanwhile, demand was also coming from the government. The Federal Aid Highways Act of 1956 provided a massive public works program. It used a new gasoline tax (raising it from 2 to 3 cents per gallon) to raise $26 billion to finance forty-one thousand miles of four-lane highways crisscrossing the United States from north to south and east to west. Not only did the program provide jobs, but it also cut the cost of transporting goods across the country. Over time, the highway system is estimated to have raised US productivity by 25 percent.[45]

One other feature of the golden age economy is worth mentioning. An expanded government, armed with the theories of Keynesian economics, felt able to minimize the cycles of a capitalist economy that had been so destructive in the prewar era. Business cycles continued (at least six between 1945 and 1975 according to the National Bureau of Economic Research, the official arbiter of US business cycles), but they were fewer, shallower, and thus less disruptive of the middle class. In fact, business cycles became something mostly affecting companies—their investment levels and inventory accumulation—rather than households. Total middle-class consumption in the United States declined only once during the golden age, in 1958.

The application of new technologies, a huge investment in education, and government's investment in infrastructure and ability to fine-tune economic policy to limit the effects of business cycles all helped America's consumer-oriented, free-market capitalism to deliver a massive expansion of the middle class. Its affluence was so great that the middle class saw little need for either a major welfare state or a collective organization of most workers into unions. The few unions that existed were able to ensure a decent living standard for their members, but they never accounted for much more than a third of the workforce. American unions were also occupied by massive infighting. The most important unions of the time, the International Brotherhood of Teamsters, the

American Federation of Labor, and the Congress of Industrial Organizations competed for influence and, in the case of the Teamsters, saw their leaders becoming embroiled in organized crime.

Unlike their European counterparts, most American unions were small and very sector-specific, such as Local 338 of the Bakery and Confectionery Workers, which controlled who could work in bagel factories. This group of some three hundred Jewish workers on Long Island, New York, was able to convert bagel baking from a hot, miserable, and dirty job to a sought-after occupation that provided enough income to pay for homes, new cars, and college educations for the children of employees. The job was even passed down from father to son, in a classic example of union power, but this power was very narrow. Like Local 338, even the large American unions had limited national power outside their own industries.

Government's role was also held in check in a nod to individual responsibility. For some observers, the limited role of the American state was a source of concern. In 1958, Harvard economist John Kenneth Galbraith wrote his treatise *The Affluent Society*, describing the dangers of excessive consumerism, where new demands are created by "advertisers . . . and the machinery for consumer-demand creation."[46] Galbraith urged the state to play a greater role in creating a new middle class of teachers, professors, surgeons, and engineers rather than an artificial middle class of corporate middle management striving to buy the latest fad consumer product.

Ironically, America would reject the idea of a larger role for the state domestically but actively support a large state role in Europe through US financing of the Marshall Plan. This plan was a generous transfer of $13.3 billion from the US government to European governments over three and a half years, an amount representing 2 percent of America's gross national income (GNI) at the time (almost seven times more than the current US ratio of foreign assistance to national income), for use in rebuilding infrastructure, fostering trade, and combating communism in war-affected European countries. It was a plan to export the American dream of a middle-class society to Europe, but it was implemented in a distinctly European fashion.

Rebuilding the European Middle Class

The United Kingdom received one-quarter of the Marshall Plan's dollars and used this money to fund a new social contract with substantially expanded government programs. As early as 1942, the coalition Conservative-Labor government in Britain, which had united to fight the war, commissioned a study of Britain's social programs. Led by a liberal economist, William Beveridge, the commission issued a report that put forward recommendations for a "comprehensive policy of social progress" to tackle the "five giant evils" of want, disease, ignorance, squalor, and idleness. Many of the report's recommendations were later enacted into law by the postwar Labor government.[47] Family allowances, national insurance, the National Health Service, rent control, and public housing were introduced. Britain aspired to have a government-sponsored welfare state that mixed democracy, capitalism, and the right to minimum living standards and services.

Britain's postwar economic success was far from guaranteed. The country emerged from the war with a massive public debt-to-GDP ratio of 230 percent, and through its new social contract, $4 out of every $10 spent in Britain for most of the next quarter century would come from the government's exchequer. But growth was reasonably high, averaging more than 2.5 percent per year, driven by trade, the introduction of new technologies, and solid employment growth. Unemployment was held below 2 percent for most of the 1950s and 1960s, and demand for labor was so strong that Britain encouraged immigration, mostly from its former colonies. Like the United States, Britain's investment in education paid off in higher wages and productivity growth, and as in the United States, postwar economic recessions were kept relatively shallow.

Yet not all was well. High tax rates and deteriorating worker-management industrial relations seemed to sap individual effort; in the 1950s and 1960s, top income tax rates reached 90 percent. The National Union of Mineworkers went on strike in 1969 to demand higher wages and shorter working hours for surface workers, who were relatively underpaid. A major follow-up strike in 1972 turned violent at the "Battle of Saltley Gate." One miner on a picket line was run over by a lorry and killed, and there were several injuries. With no coal, electricity supply to the grid had to be rationed, and high-risk areas saw several hours of brownouts. Millions of industrial workers lost their jobs. After the strike was broken, a government inquiry led by an independent British judge, Lord Wilberforce, recommended a pay raise of 27 percent for the miners, which was finally accepted.

The British experience of the 1970s was a stark reminder of how political fissures could develop even within the middle class. Miners were well paid compared to other industrial workers, although their jobs were dangerous. But the miners' relative pay had steadily eroded as economic vibrancy moved toward London and the south, where professionals and service-sector earners were finding more opportunity and where market forces had driven up earnings. The geographic divide within Britain was accentuated by a perceived loss of relative standing between Britain and other European countries—including Germany and Italy, which had lost the war but seemed to be winning the economic benefits of the peace. While strong, Britain's postwar growth lagged behind its continental neighbors. When oil prices suddenly increased in 1973, Britain plunged into a two-year recession. It did not matter that by 1975, nine out of ten British families enjoyed middle-class lifestyles. Relatively speaking, they were falling behind or at least seeing their economic advantages slipping away. Britain's social contract would need to be revisited.

On the European continent, the new social contract involved an even stronger role for the state. Before the war, the European middle class was still firmly rooted in small businesses, often in rural areas and small towns. These places were devastated by war. Families lost their savings because of inflation. Destroyed roads and bridges made even internal domestic trade difficult.

But there was opportunity in the destruction—a chance to build anew in an egalitarian way. The advantages of wealth, which had previously limited social mobility for those without it, were replaced by opportunities for self-advancement based on hard work and individual achievement. The precise mechanisms differed by country, but there were common threads. Europe went through a period of rapid transformation of the labor force into wage earners, especially in professional service sectors, middle management, and the civil service. The share of self-employed people in the labor force fell fast. Demand for economic goods and services was maintained by government spending, including for infrastructure reconstruction, and by wage and employment growth, with a postwar baby boom providing an extra accelerator.

It is worth remembering what living conditions were like in Europe shortly after the war. For example, in France in the mid-1950s, more than a third of households lacked running water and less than one-fifth had a bath or shower. Household appliances, like refrigerators and washing machines, were even more scarce—luxuries that only 10 to 20 percent of households could afford. Few families had cars. So it was relatively easy to predict what consumers wanted. The challenge was to produce the goods at reasonable cost and quality and to ensure that enough households had sufficient income to buy them.

It was governments that helped match production to consumption and that organized the process of "catch-up" growth, so called because Europe strove to achieve American levels of productivity by copying the technologies and business models used in the United States. In France, which had a relatively large rural population, labor productivity was boosted by huge investments in tractors and agricultural machinery under a plan developed for the French government by the planning commissioner, Jean Monnet. Output per person in French agriculture rose by 7 percent per year as the number of tractors and combine harvesters grew twentyfold in two decades.

France became the most state-controlled capitalist country in the world during this period of *Les Trentes Glorieuses*, thirty years of postwar growth at 5 percent per year, equivalent to the quadrupling of average incomes in a generation. Coal, electricity, gas, airlines, banks, and even Renault, the car company, were owned by the state. The state also helped develop cities to handle the population exodus from rural areas, as well as the new households being formed by baby boomers. Construction surged ahead to modernize the housing stock, which was old, dilapidated, and damaged by war.

Unions played a major role in French reconstruction, as they had during the Resistance as well. In some instances, workers took over the management of factories whose owners were found to have collaborated with the Nazis. Regardless of ownership, works committees were set up in every large business; these committees were empowered to deal with labor issues such as safety concerns and hours worked, as well as to review the profitability and productivity of the enterprise and to ensure that workers' interests were properly addressed.

The workers organized themselves into unions with a matrix structure: by industry at the national level and by geography at the local level. Thus, each locality in France had several unions, one for each industry, which coordinated among themselves locally while coordinating with other members of the same industry nationally. This structure permitted wages to be set in a systematic way across the country. A base wage was established by the National Wages Committee and then adjustments were made for skill level, hazard, and other considerations, such as local cost-of-living differences.

The German experience with reconstruction was somewhat different. Germany had lost the war, was effectively divided into two countries—West and East—and was on the front line of the new Cold War between capitalists and communists. West Germany had a reasonably intact base of machine tools and industrial capital at war's end. However, the Allies decided at the Potsdam Conference that the new German economy should be based on agriculture and light industry. Accordingly, many West German heavy-industry factories were physically removed by the British and American forces and relocated to those countries as reparations for the cost of the war.

By 1950, the strategy changed. Germany was viewed as a strategic ally of the West, and German industrialization was seen as key to the recovery of Europe's economy. French foreign minister Robert Schuman proposed a new plan creating the European Coal and Steel Community, which would regulate industrial production in its six member countries, including France and Germany. The basis of the plan was that economically integrated countries would have a great disincentive to fight among themselves. The Franco-German axis that remains at the heart of the European Union (EU) today was born, and with it, the idea that peace was fundamental to middle-class interests. So novel was this seemingly obvious idea that the Nobel Prize Committee honored the EU in 2012 with its Peace Prize for transforming Europe from a continent of conflict to a continent of peace while simultaneously working to advance peace across the world.

In many ways, German reconstruction followed that of other countries in Europe, with the twist that the German version featured strength in industrial production, specifically in cars. In Hitler's time, Germany had introduced the Volkswagen (VW) Beetle, the people's car, as a vehicle specially designed with the middle class in mind. The Beetle was affordable, practical, and reliable—just what was needed in the postwar era. Many Beetles were exported to other countries, allowing VW to drive down costs even further through economies of scale and to pass these savings on to its customers. By 1972, the VW Beetle had become the best-selling car of all time, with more than fifteen million units sold, beating the forty-year record held by Ford's Model T.[48]

The German economic miracle was built on some unique designs aimed at fostering a sense of equality and shared sacrifice. The German social market economy was a deliberate mix of free markets with a strong voice of labor and a strong welfare state. Unlike Anglo-Saxon models of the welfare state, which were championed by labor movements and left-leaning political parties, the German model was rooted in the conservative Christian Democratic Party, which ran every government from 1949 to 1969. The social market economy was so popular that it was also embraced by the liberal Social Democratic Party in 1959. With both major political parties endorsing the fundamentals of a social market economy, political debate was about efficient implementation, not policy direction.

The three pillars of the German social market economy were American-style free markets, the welfare state as newly formed in Britain, and the works councils and labor representation in business that developed in parallel in France and Germany. The importance of this last pillar was in ensuring that business profits were shared with workers. The works councils were represented on big business boards, had access to firms' financial information, and coordinated themselves at national levels in sectors that could negotiate wage agreements. Taking their cue from the leading metal workers union, other major industrial sectors could follow its path, obviating the need for national collective bargaining or a national minimum wage. In 1960, 85 percent of German workers were covered by collective bargaining agreements, which used national productivity growth as a key input.[49]

The commitment to equality in Germany was also seen in a large welfare state funded by progressive taxes. In 1952, the German government introduced a wealth tax, essentially confiscating half of everything that people owned in 1949, but with a wrinkle: the tax was to be paid over thirty years, in 120 installments of 0.4166 percent each quarter, allowing for most of the tax to be paid out of new profits. This burden sharing meant that most households' well-being resulted from their own efforts, with little impact from any inheritance. It was a great leveler, contributing to a new middle class with a strong culture of duty, responsibility, egalitarianism, conformism, and discipline. In everything from lifestyle to education, the objective was to allow as many people as possible to share in the benefits of economic growth and to consume in moderation individually but on a large scale collectively. Lavish consumption was frowned upon; the postwar German idea of the good life was to be able to travel to Italy by car to soak up the sun for a few weeks of vacation each year.

Each country in Europe pursued its own version of a new social contract. One much-discussed model is the Scandinavian (or more properly, Nordic, to include Finland, Iceland, and Greenland, in addition to Denmark, Norway, and Sweden) model that emerged from reforms that were put in place even before the war in response to the economic crisis generated by the Great Depression. Because the Nordic countries had instituted a democratic system of proportional representation that encouraged coalition building across parties and between labor and capital, they had already worked out a balance of state-provided education, health, and other services, state ownership of key companies, and centralized wage negotiations. For example, although Norway has a market economy, its government still owns many natural resource companies in petroleum, gas, timber, water, fish, and minerals, accounting for one-quarter of all sales in the country. This system proved ideally suited to the postwar desire for stability and social harmony and was reliably rewarded by middle-class voters. Sweden's postwar prime minister, Tage Erlander, served continuously in his post for twenty-three years, from 1946 until 1969, and was then replaced by his protege, Olof Palme, for another seven years. This kind of stability for thirty years is rather unusual in a democratic system and clearly works well for Nordic countries—they routinely rank at the top of the list of the countries with the happiest citizens in the world—but it is not easy for other countries to emulate this success because their middle-class politics play out in such different ways.

Cracks in the Western Middle-Class Model

Sometime around 1975, the size of the global middle class first surpassed one billion people. It had taken about 150 years since the beginnings of the Industrial Revolution, with many a detour along the way, but by the mid-1970s, the United States, Canada, Australia, most of Europe, and Japan had created economic systems with almost everyone—85 to 95 percent of households—in the middle class. This does not mean there were not significant and severe inequalities. The middle class is very wide, and the gap between the top and the bottom of the class is large. But most people had opportunities for a decent life with many of the essentials of a healthy and comfortable existence, and the middle class had established itself as the dominant force in domestic politics in advanced economies.

Yet all was not well in these societies, and the social contract started to unravel in the face of economic pressures. In some places, there was growing resentment against the stifling effects of government regulation. In Nordic countries and the United Kingdom, high taxes, large public sector deficits and trade imbalances were making the welfare state increasingly unaffordable. In the United States, inflation had started to rise with the pursuit of the war in Vietnam, and the US dollar—the mainstay of international finance and trade—came under pressure. European countries that were running trade surpluses with the United States were asking to be paid in gold rather than in US dollars. In 1971, President Richard Nixon severed the convertibility of the US dollar into gold at the then-fixed price of $35 per ounce. All the industrialized countries were hard hit by the decision of oil producers to raise their prices in

1973. A period of "stagflation"—stagnant economic growth coupled with high inflation—followed, worsened by policy mistakes of central bankers who mistakenly tightened monetary policy to combat higher inflation, as they had done in the past when high demand had caused inflation, without realizing that this was the wrong approach to take in the face of a supply shock.

In short, just when the middle class reached a truly global scale with hitherto undreamed-of prosperity for households living in industrialized countries, the social contract in the West started to fray. A new era of globalization was about to start—one that would integrate many more countries into a global web of trade, foreign investment, international capital flows, and immigration. The Western middle class would need to find a way to continue to prosper in a very different economic environment.

~

Chapter 3

THE SECOND BILLION

Economic Growth in the Third World and Globalization, 1975–2006

> The consequences for human welfare involved in questions like these [policy actions to raise economic growth] are simply staggering: once one starts to think about them, it is hard to think about anything else.
>
> —Robert Lucas Jr., Nobel Laureate in Economics, 1988[1]

In the mid-1970s, the world was divided into three groups of countries. The first world consisted of the advanced industrialized economies of the West, with strong economic and military ties with each other through the North Atlantic Treaty Organization (NATO) and the Organization for Economic Cooperation and Development (OECD), founded in 1949 and 1961, respectively. The second world consisted of communist countries that largely traded with each other and, in the case of European socialist republics, formed part of the Warsaw Pact military alliance and the Council for Mutual Economic Assistance. The third world consisted of countries that were not aligned with either of these groups and that were generally economically poor. Three-quarters of the world's population, more than three billion people, lived in third world countries in 1975, and very few of these third-world citizens were in the global middle class.

By 1975, the gap in living standards between people living in the first and second worlds compared with the third world was the largest it had ever been in human history. People in the first world almost universally were able to afford a middle-class lifestyle. Remember that according to the definition used in this book, there is a tenfold difference between the top and bottom of the middle-class range, so significant inequalities still existed in these countries. But extreme poverty had largely been eradicated. The same was true in most of the second world, although people were substantially less well-off compared to first world countries and also did not have the freedom of choice that is central to the concept of being middle class. In the third world, however, most people were still desperately poor. Their societies had none of the characteristics that underpinned the middle class in the West. Seven out of ten people lived in rural areas, and most were illiterate. Any economic gains were eroded by rapid population growth, so individual household incomes per person stayed low. In addition, it cost a lot to transport goods to the major markets of the West, and there were few factories with modern machinery, so industrialization was slow to take off.

Why was a large, prosperous middle class something that only existed in European countries and their offshoots in 1975? Was it just a matter of time, of waiting for developing countries to catch up, or was it something more intrinsic to cultures, societies, and politics? Was a large Western middle class dependent on exploiting overseas colonies? Would developing countries mimic the development pathways of advanced countries or develop quite different paths with a different type of middle class? These were the major questions that Nobel laureate Bob Lucas raised in his quest to understand the dynamics of economic growth in the world.

For about thirty years, starting around 1975, there was a Great Convergence of living standards among countries. This was a period of globalization, of a rapid expansion of international trade, and of cross-border flows of capital; a period when most countries gave up on populist and nationalist programs in favor of more orthodox economic management summarized by a set of principles that the American economist John Williamson would dub the Washington Consensus; and a period when the fall of the Berlin Wall literally removed the barrier between the first and second worlds. During the Great Convergence, the middle class spread around the world to Asia, Latin America, and Eastern Europe. In doing so, the pace of middle-class expansion started to accelerate; it had taken the rich world 150 years to move a billion people into the middle class. The second billion would be added in just thirty-one years, from 1975 to 2006.

Globalization, the East Asian Miracle, and the Growth of Asia's Middle Class

After World War II, Japan's economy was in shambles, with industrial output reduced to a quarter of the prewar level and an average income less than one-tenth that of the United States. Hardly any Japanese households could be classified as middle class. Subsequently, thirty years of rapid economic growth totally transformed Japan, and by 1975 it had become the only non-Western country with a majority of its population in the middle class. Japan achieved this in much the same way as Europe, through a heavy emphasis on industrialization.

For neighboring Asian countries, Japan became the model to emulate. It exemplified a linear evolution of how modernization would foster economic growth. Economic growth would create a middle class. A middle class would vote for a government that focused its efforts on modernization and economic growth. This closed cycle would provide the blueprint for a prosperous society.

In the Japanese model, the "salaryman" became the iconic symbol of the new middle class. The salaryman was a lifelong employee of a large corporation, devoted to its economic success. He was well educated, worked long hours, and socialized with colleagues to build corporate spirit. Unlike many breadwinners in the Western middle class, the Japanese head of a middle-class household put work and the corporation ahead of personal enjoyment and family life.

Elites in other Asian countries found the Japanese model attractive. For the political class, Japan showed a way of combining democracy with one-party rule. The Japanese Liberal Democratic Party maintained the premiership every year from 1955 until 1993. For the corporate elite, the Japanese model was built on industrial champions and conglomerates supported by the government. There were, of course, debates about the lessons to be drawn from Japan: Was it government intervention or private industry that mattered? How important was the provision of cheap and plentiful finance? Should the coordinated expansion of business houses through plans drawn up by Japan's powerful Ministry of International Trade and Industry be mimicked by others? These details have been debated by economic historians but the overarching idea of linking modernization, economic growth, development of the middle class, and national politics into a single program was taken up by other East Asian countries, starting with South Korea, Taiwan, and the city-states of Hong Kong and Singapore, and continuing with Indonesia, Malaysia, and Thailand. These countries were known as high-performing Asian economies because they managed to achieve strong economic growth at rates that even exceeded the speed of advanced economy growth over long periods of at least a generation.

The high-performing Asian economies followed an economic pathway similar to Japan's, the parallels so close that Japanese economist Kaname Akamatsu dubbed this pathway the "flying geese model." The core idea was that Japan, as the lead goose, showed the way for other countries. As Japanese industry moved up the ladder of technological sophistication, it would move out of simpler industries, leaving a space in the global marketplace that other countries could move into. In the 1960s, Japan moved out of garments, textiles, and light manufactures (for example, toys, shoes) and instead focused on heavy industry (automobiles, shipbuilding, steel, chemicals, and machine tools). South Korea and Taiwan were then able to take over light manufacturing exports before starting their own move to heavy industry in the 1980s. As this happened, Malaysia, Indonesia, and Thailand took over production of garments, semiconductors, and other light manufactures.

Through this model of industrialization, several Asian countries were able to grow rapidly at the same time, each with advantages in specific industries. The process of technological upgrading and restructuring required significant investments in plants and machinery, willingly supplied by Western and north Asian companies.

The flying geese model provided a framework for understanding how countries could sequentially develop technological capabilities and shift focus from low value-adding industries to higher value-adding industries. Harvard economist Ricardo Haussman has formalized this process by developing what he calls the Atlas of Economic Complexity—a listing, by industrial product, of items that are most difficult to master from a technological point of view. The atlas shows the pathways that countries have taken as they move up the ladder of technological complexity toward industries that can support the highest-wage jobs.[2] With this model, however, it becomes hard for countries to leapfrog others because they have to go through the process of acquiring existing technology before taking the next step. In Asia, it did not always go as planned. The lead goose, Japan, was unable to continually upgrade its productivity levels, and Japanese living standards have now been surpassed by those in Taiwan, Hong Kong, South Korea, and Singapore.

The Asian growth model, in Japan and elsewhere, relied on keeping wage rates well below the levels of advanced economies. This structure, however, was untenable, causing the United States, in particular, to suffer a decrease in manufacturing jobs from a peak level of 19.4 million in October 1979 to 16.8 million in April 1983.[3] In response, the US government called for a meeting to discuss the situation. In September 1985, officials from the United States, Japan, France, the United Kingdom, and West Germany—the five largest economies in the world at the time—met at the Plaza Hotel in New York City and agreed to ask their central banks to pursue policies that would permit a large depreciation of the US dollar, making wages in foreign countries more expensive in dollar terms.

The impact of the "Plaza Accord" was immediate and dramatic. The Japanese yen, which had been trading at around 240 to the US dollar in 1985, quickly rose to a value of ¥150 per dollar, and by 1988 had risen to ¥120 per dollar, exactly twice its pre-accord value.

With a single stroke of the pen, the Plaza Accord put Japan's need to restructure its industry on steroids by doubling the US dollar cost of Japanese wages. Smaller Asian countries kept their currencies fixed against the dollar, so they suddenly enjoyed a huge cost advantage that they would take full advantage of. It helped that entire factories could be re-created in virtually any location. The same buildings and layout could be constructed anywhere, the machinery imported, and even supervisors and managers could be transplanted from home offices. The main requirements for success were the ability to get inputs to the factory quickly and efficiently, to have a disciplined workforce, and to get the goods being produced to markets abroad at reasonable cost. This called for good infrastructure and for efficient government agencies, especially those handling customs, business permits, and work visas. The high-performing Asian economies provided these services.

The bulk of Asian exports during this period went to satisfy the demands of the Western middle class. The Swedish retailer IKEA is an example of a company that took advantage of globalization to expand. IKEA's vision is to "create a better everyday life for many people—for customers, but also for our co-workers and the people who work at our suppliers."[4] Two things make IKEA the quintessential middle-class company: its products are inexpensive so that many people can afford them, and they are well designed and functional, so they are suited to middle-class families. The famous flat pack—IKEA's ingenious idea to slash storage and transport costs by boxing all components, with the final product to be assembled by the purchaser—allowed IKEA to source from anywhere in the world and to bring costs down by expanding volume.

There are innumerable companies like IKEA in every consumer goods industry in the world. These industries cater to individuals and households rather than to other businesses as their core customers. The industries differentiate themselves through marketing, advertising, and branding, and they use technology to keep costs low and to develop new consumer preferences. For instance, Uniqlo, a Japanese clothing company, does not see itself as a fashion company but as a technology company. Its Heattech fabric turns moisture into heat, which is retained in small air pockets in the fibers. This allows the company to make warm clothes that are thin and stylish rather than bulky.

The IKEA and Uniqlo examples show how the middle class in advanced economies and in developing East Asia are intertwined but very different in nature. In the new global value chains that these companies represent, high-wage jobs in innovation, design, branding, marketing, and finance have been created in the West, while cheap labor in manufacturing provides jobs and incomes in the East.

This model has worked spectacularly well for both groups. Consumer goods were produced in Asia in quantities far larger than their own small domestic markets would have supported. Economic growth accelerated to rates that had not been seen during peacetime anywhere in the world. In East Asia, exports soared from 20 percent to 60 percent of gross domestic product between the 1960s and the 2000s. As a comparison, US exports stayed steady at around 10 percent during this time; Germany, one of the leading exporter countries in the world, had a 30 percent share of its economy in exports in 2000.

Thanks to rapid economic growth and constant improvements in technology, Asian countries could steadily increase wages for decade upon decade. This was not driven by organized labor, but by a political elite that viewed political and social stability as an essential ingredient of a business friendly environment. Indeed, all the high-performing Asian economies enjoyed considerable political stability. There were democratic elections, to be sure, yet the same single party governed for long periods during the growth spurt in Indonesia (1967–1998), Taiwan (1948–2000), Malaysia (1957–2018), and Singapore (1959–present).

What kept these governments in power was the promise to transform their impoverished societies into places where the middle class could flourish. A unique feature of East Asian growth was that income became more equally distributed as affluence rose. This experience was quite different from what had occurred during the years of unfettered capitalist growth in the United States in the 1920s, for example, when huge inequalities in income were visibly apparent and ultimately caused the Great Depression. Growth with equity in East Asia was not accidental nor due to any change in the way that capitalism operated. Rather, it was caused by intentional government policy.

Across East Asia, governments took it upon themselves to educate their people. Education has long been revered in the region. Some scholars trace this back 2,500 years to the tradition of Confucianism. Confucius emphasized education as the bedrock not just of individual success but of a flourishing family, community, and even world. He believed that all people are born equal and that everyone can and should be educated and learn how to continuously learn throughout their lives.

All the high-performing Asian economies had major government policies to provide education, initially at primary and secondary levels, but increasingly at the tertiary level. A crucial element of Asian success that is less well-known in the rest of the world is the ability to rapidly raise education levels. Indeed, many Asian countries have surpassed the United States in the average learning outcome of their workers and the percentage of workers who achieve minimum proficiency benchmarks to make them productive.[5]

Simple literacy helped transform self-employed rural farmers into wage-earning industrial workers. Even those who stayed behind on the farm saw rapid increases in their incomes. Indeed, although East Asia is most famous for its exports of manufactured goods during this period, an unsung but enormously impactful part of its success was its ability to raise agricultural productivity and growth to previously unheard-of levels, thanks to the application of modern fertilizers, seeds, and mechanization by educated farmers.

In East Asia, educational attainment has become a status symbol. Several countries conduct national examinations at the end of high school. The results determine which students get into the top universities. Naturally there is massive pressure to do well, so in countries like South Korea, for example, private tutors are regularly hired to prepare teenagers for these exams. The best teachers are like national rock stars—they lecture in large stadiums, earn millions of dollars a year, and have a cultlike following among their students.[6]

The Asian education system provides a mechanism for sorting people into a social hierarchical order that is quite different from that in the West. National examinations provide measurable results along a single scale. Because the top students on this ranking get into the best universities, they emerge with the best prospects for high-wage jobs. So the examination rankings translate into income and consumption rankings and become good proxies for identifying where students will fall on the economic spectrum later in life.

The huge societal transformations that took place in East Asia—from rural to urban societies, from farm to industrial work, from self-employment to wage-earning labor—offered opportunities for women as well as men. Anyone walking into an Asian garment factory in the 1980s was immediately struck by the scene of row upon row of young women sitting at sewing machines. The only men were the shop-floor supervisors, usually tucked against the wall of a huge open floor plan hangar.

With both men and women working in factories, a new social structure emerged seemingly overnight: households with two wage earners. The impact was enormous. These households had more income and could afford the houses, cars (or at least motorcycles), and appliances that Western middle-class consumers routinely bought for themselves. But the indirect effects were even more important. Most garment factory workers started work at around age seventeen. These young women chose to delay marriage so they could work and be independent. They waited to have their first child so the family could save more. They had fewer children with longer spacing between them. With more income and fewer children, these women could afford to spend more on each child's education and health.

Two-income families in East Asia exhibited all the traditional characteristics of a middle-class life: hard work and individual responsibility to improve the life of their families, thrift and saving to permit purchases of homes and consumer durables like cars, and the ability and desire to educate their children and to create an upwardly mobile society.

Across East Asia, almost half of women seventeen and older started to work, even in Muslim countries like Malaysia and Indonesia. In comparison, when the United States' middle class was already mature in the 1930s, only 22 percent of adult women worked outside the home. The US and European middle classes were enabled by high wages paid to the head of household. In East Asia, the middle class was characterized by the prevalence of two-income households, with each earner making a comparatively low wage.

Governments helped the process of attracting women into the wage-earning labor force by actively recruiting women into the civil service. Large government programs to expand education and health hired many women as teachers and nurses. The recipe for successful growth of the middle class was complete: low taxes, plentiful jobs for both men and women, wage increases linked to technological upgrading, public provision of health, education, and low-cost housing, and well-planned improvements in infrastructure to ensure cheap and reliable connectivity with global markets.

The East Asian model was not perfect. Its Achilles' heel was debt. Economic growth rates in Indonesia, South Korea, Malaysia, Taiwan,

Thailand, and Singapore were in the high single-digit range, and each country recorded at least one year of double-digit growth. At these levels, the economies were doubling in size every nine or ten years. The level of credit growth was even more rapid and was supplied by borrowing from abroad, much of which was from Japanese banks, mostly requiring repayment in US dollars. The credits were exposed to exchange rate risk.

In the mid-1990s, the economy in the United States was starting to overheat as it rebounded from recession. Fearing a return of inflation, the US Federal Reserve Board raised interest rates, and the US dollar started to rise in value. This affected the balance sheet of Japanese banks. When converted back into yen, the value of their outstanding dollar loans to Asian countries became much larger and too big to be supported by their small levels of equity. The Japanese banks needed to retrench, and in a relatively short period, they started to call in their dollar loans. Asian borrowers were faced with an acute dollar shortage.

Whenever there are stresses to financial markets, speculators move in quickly to take advantage. The billionaire investor George Soros read the tea leaves correctly and predicted that Asian countries would have to devalue their currencies. His fund, along with many others, sold Asian currencies short. The rest, as they say, is history. Starting with the collapse of the Thai baht in July 1997, currency crises spread to Malaysia, Indonesia, and South Korea, revealing structural weaknesses in the economies. Real estate developers, for example, were hugely overextended. Property markets collapsed, ushering in a wave of corporate and financial institution bankruptcies. The economic declines exceeded those recorded in advanced economies during the Great Depression. The Indonesian economy in 1998, for example, suffered a 40 percent decline in a single year when measured in US dollars.

Astonishingly, Asian policymakers did not abandon their economic model of promoting private-sector, export-oriented businesses with open trade and capital markets. (One exception was Malaysia, which temporarily imposed capital controls, but only after most of the foreign "hot money" had already left the country.) Instead, they fixed their banks, restructured companies, and introduced even stronger market competition. The middle class took a substantial hit as wages and employment dropped steeply. Yet globalization was such a powerful force that, within a decade, the effects of the Asian Financial Crisis already were overcome, and the Asian economies had returned to their previous path of rapid growth, with equity and a steadily strengthening middle class.

In South Korea, the country that managed the Asian crisis most successfully, the middle class took it upon themselves to save the economy. An estimated one-quarter of the population contributed jewelry, coins, watches, medals, and other gold items that were commonly found in middle-class Korean households to help pay off the national debt. Companies and celebrities spearheaded the drive. More than $2.2 billion was collected in this way—a sizable fraction of the $11 billion of long-term debt owed by the government in 1997.

Despite the setback during the crisis years, South Korea was able to build its middle class from 12 percent of its population in 1975 to 90 percent by the year 2000. In other words, in a single generation spanning about twenty-five years, the country achieved the same improvement in the size of its middle class as the United States had done in one hundred years. Progress in other countries was not as dramatic as this example of South Korea, but it was still far more rapid than in advanced economies due to the impact of globalization.

The result was that by 2006, there were more than 420 million East Asians among the global middle class, with 300 million of them living outside Japan. Less than one-fifth of the East Asian middle class lived in mainland China, which, after many years of economic reforms, was just starting to establish its own domestic market. The bulk lived in South Korea, Taiwan, Hong Kong, and the countries of Southeast Asia that had embraced globalization.

Yet this Asian middle class was very different from that in the West. The Western middle class grew on the backs of small businesses, self-employment, and, especially in Europe, strong unions and powerful wage bargaining. In East Asia, the middle class was made up of the salary men and women working for large companies and forming educated (but relatively underpaid) two-income households. In the West, the middle class often strove to restrict the size of government to keep taxes low. In East Asia, the middle class was fully dependent on a government that prioritized economic growth above all else. The Western middle class was different from other classes and, despite its name, not considered to be inferior to the rich. The East Asian middle class was literally the middle of a strict hierarchical ranking as exemplified by national examinations, and from this perspective, it ranked as inferior to the upper class. And although consumption patterns followed the same trajectory in West and East—homes, cars, furniture, vacations, education, health, and entertainment—the nature of the middle class was quite different.

The Washington Consensus and the Growth of the Latin American Middle Class

At the same time that East Asian exports were taking off, there was an ongoing debate in the rest of the world about the role of government in economic development. The precise contribution of the Asian governments' industrial policies was contentious, but there was broad agreement on the importance of other fundamentals: low taxes; avoidance of inflation; pro-growth public spending on education, health, and infrastructure; competitive interest and exchange rates; openness to trade and foreign investment; and the primacy of private business, guided by reasonable regulations, prudent oversight of financial institutions, and secure property rights.

This list had been drawn up by the American economist John Williamson, a longtime researcher of development processes in Latin American countries.[7] Williamson's list derived largely from the failures of Latin American countries that had ignored one or more of these precepts and that had consequently failed to grow fast. He tried to convey the idea that there was a set of basic fundamentals every country should sensibly follow and that the reason why so many Latin American countries failed to live up to their development potential was that they had not implemented what he called "motherhood and apple pie" policies.[8] Williamson called his list the Washington Consensus[9] because these policies were always part of the advice given to developing country governments by the major development agencies in Washington, DC, the International Monetary Fund and the World Bank. But he regretted that name to his dying day because it reeked of colonialism and of conditions being imposed on Latin American governments rather than conveying lessons learned by Latin American economists. Williamson always viewed the Washington Consensus as a policy package of necessary conditions for sustained economic growth that was based on conclusions drawn by Latin American government officials as they reflected on their experiences suffering through a major debt crisis in the mid-1980s. Why, they asked, had a region that was so rich in natural resources failed to develop rapidly?

One reason the economists offered was that most Latin American governments had poor control over public finances, spending heavily on government salaries and leaving little for the provision of needed services, like health and education, or for infrastructure. As a consequence, Latin American countries had some of the most unequal distributions of income anywhere in the world. A few lucky people had jobs in government, multinational companies, or large domestic corporations, while the rest were left to fend for themselves. Periodic bouts of high inflation eroded any savings the middle class might have and kept these countries from developing further.

A second reason was that many Latin American governments still owned state enterprises that ran large parts of the countries' economies, usually in very inefficient ways. These inefficiencies rippled down throughout those economies. If electricity and water supply are expensive and unreliable, then it is hard for firms to be competitive. Large firms can often work around these problems—by having their own power generators, for example—but small and medium-sized firms cannot.

A third reason was that insufficient attention was paid to economic institutions. Among the most problematic institutions were labor markets. Latin America had formidable unions that kept wages high and tried to ensure employment stability for their members. The price the countries paid was that not enough jobs were created, and so, ironically, most workers were pushed into an informal labor market where they had few rights, poor working conditions, and no ability to negotiate wage increases.

A recent study by the McKinsey Global Institute (MGI) looked back at the structural reasons for Latin America's relatively poor performance and concluded that it has had a long history of two "missing middles"—mid-sized companies and middle-class households.[10] When comparing Latin American industry with that of well-performing countries, MGI concluded that in Latin America there were many small, inefficient firms and a few large corporations. What was missing was a layer of dynamic, medium-sized firms that could provide good jobs and productive opportunities for domestic entrepreneurs. Without such medium-sized firms, Latin America lacked innovation and an ability to adopt new technologies.

The other big difference between Latin America and high-performing countries that MGI focused on was the absence of a large cohort of middle-class consumers who could afford new products, drive demand, and provide an incentive for firms to invest more. The proportion of domestic consumption in Latin America accounted for by top earners was the highest in the world.

The two missing middles are interrelated. The missing middle of firms reduces the number of good wage-paying jobs and contributes to a large informal sector and a missing middle of consumers. Conversely, a missing middle of consumers reduces demand for new products and innovations and contributes to the missing middle of dynamic medium-sized firms that could respond to domestic demand.

This has become the trap into which Latin American economies have fallen. By and large, people are not desperately poor in the way that poverty reveals itself in Africa and some parts of South Asia, but they are not well off either, and, most importantly, they are stuck. Many Latin American countries fall into what is called the "middle-income trap." This is a situation in which countries have wages that are too high relative to the productivity of workers to permit the countries to compete on global export markets for industrial goods, and at the same time domestic firms are not sufficiently dynamic to innovate and absorb the best technologies from abroad.

When caught in this trap, countries rely on their natural resource wealth to survive, and this is one area in which Latin America is well endowed. Farmers in Brazil, Argentina, and Chile are world leaders in the production of soybeans, citrus, and wine. Colombia is known the world over for its coffee, as is Peru for the fish in its local waters. Latin America has oil and precious metals. All these resources allow for a standard of living that can support a mid-sized middle class, but as yet no Latin American country has been able to lift anything close to 90 percent of its people into the middle class as South Korea has done. (Uruguay comes closest with 80 to 85 percent of its population now in the middle class.)

With middle-class fortunes tied to natural resources, either directly because this is where people work or indirectly because government jobs and salaries reflect the ability of Latin American governments to tax their natural resource sectors, middle-class households in Latin America are exposed to the ups and downs of global commodity markets. In the late 1970s, commodities were on an upswing, and oil and food prices rose substantially. After peaking around 1980, however, commodity prices fell steadily for almost two decades.

It is no accident that food prices and crude oil prices move together. Petrochemicals derived from crude oil are a major ingredient in the production of fertilizer. Crude oil is also a cost factor in processing and transporting food from farm to market. In addition, both react to similar macroeconomic conditions: prices for all commodities usually rise together when demand is high, and they rise further when liquidity is high and interest rates are low, reducing the cost of storage and encouraging an accumulation of inventories.

Exposed in this way to global commodity cycles, the Latin American middle class was able to expand until 1980, then it suffered through a lost decade up to the early 1990s before beginning a slow recovery that lasted through the early 2000s. The lost decade coincided with falling commodity prices but was driven even more directly by the aftermath of a severe debt crisis that engulfed many countries in the region, including all the major economies.

During the 1970s commodity boom, Latin American countries looked to boost their middle class through populist policies financed by foreign banks, mostly based in the United States. The banks were willing to lend because, as Walter Wriston (then chair of Citibank) is reported to have said, "countries don't go bankrupt." Wriston was not being facetious; he was making an important substantive point. Under US bankruptcy law, when a company cannot repay its debts, it can enter into a Chapter 11 process in which the company presents a plan to its creditors that, if accepted by them and approved by the court, permits the company to reorganize its affairs. There is an organized process and plan. The problem was that on the international scene, when Mexico defaulted on its foreign debt service payments in August 1982, there was no established system for preparing a coordinated plan to restructure its debt.

This is what Wriston referred to. He firmly believed that with sound policies, economic and financial management, and time enough for implementation, any country would be able to generate the foreign exchange needed to service its debt. But the plan had to be coordinated and accepted by creditors, and it needed time to work.

Creditors to Latin American countries wanted to get their money back as quickly as possible. Governments wanted a gradual adjustment. The final compromise was orchestrated by the International Monetary Fund and supported by the US Treasury (under the guidance of secretaries Jim Baker and Nicholas Brady, after whom debt restructuring plans were named). It required Latin American governments to make sharp fiscal and currency adjustments. They had to raise taxes, cut spending, and devalue their currencies, leading to inflation. The impact of these austerity programs fell primarily on the middle class. Government provision of health and education, pensions, and infrastructure investments all had to be cut. Middle-class savings were eroded by inflation—a recurrent theme in this book—and by a decrease in wages and employment.

It was against this backdrop that the Washington Consensus was developed, with its focus on sound public finances and low inflation. Though harsh in its implementation, the plan at least offered some hope for the future. By the mid-1990s, several Latin American countries were able to resume steady growth. Most had learned the lessons of fiscal discipline and avoiding crises.

By 2006, when the global middle class surpassed two billion people, almost three hundred million of them were living in Latin America, and more than half, about 175 million people, had been added to this number during the prior thirty-one years despite the debt crisis and other setbacks. Latin America had become a solidly middle-class region, with over half its population able to afford a middle-class lifestyle (and a few who were truly wealthy, even by global standards). It would not be accurate to describe the Latin American middle class as dynamic or a source of sustainable growth and development, but it had become large enough to be a potent political force. Throughout the continent, the Latin American middle class began to push for efficient government, anticorruption, and low taxes, the same basic agenda that drove the progressives in the United States at the end of the nineteenth century.

It is still unclear whether the middle class will be successful with their agenda in Latin America. Several Latin American countries have swung sharply between governments that support a capitalist agenda largely benefiting elites and governments that support populist agendas temporarily benefiting the poor. Only a few countries, such as Chile and Uruguay, have been able to develop their middle class to the same degree as South Korea.

The Fall of the Berlin Wall and the Growth of the Eastern European Middle Class

When the Berlin Wall fell on November 9, 1989, it marked the beginning of an era of opportunity for the three hundred million people then living in the Eastern Bloc. In short order, starting with Hungary and Poland in 1994, the European Union (EU) entered into interim association agreements covering one hundred million people in Central and Eastern Europe and opened the door to future membership for another one hundred million people in southeastern Europe and, more distantly, an additional seventy-five million people further to the east.[11]

It is hard to provide a good comparative understanding of living conditions in Eastern Europe and the former Soviet Union before the Berlin Wall fell, because their system of accounts was so different from that in the rest of the world. At a superficial level, there were several attributes of decent material well-being. Children were well educated, economies were industrialized, towns and cities were well established. There was good health care and education, jobs were guaranteed for men and women, and housing was provided. State-owned enterprises provided social services and safety nets. Inequality was low, although the elite enjoyed significant privileges.

Yet there was also massive inefficiency and waste. Some of this was readily visible. In Poland, for example, inflation reached such high levels toward the end of 1989 that there was a severe shortage of goods. People waited in long lines without even knowing what was being sold, based on the simple idea that there must be something more worthwhile than the currency in their pockets if others were also queuing up. There were also less visible inefficiencies, because most goods were produced at a quality and price that simply was not competitive on global markets. Sometimes this was obvious; sometimes it came as a complete surprise. For example, in the early days of perestroika, the program introduced by Soviet president Mikhail Gorbachev to move from a planned economy toward one that was more market based, the planning ministry was asked to prepare a study to determine which domestic industries were most likely to be globally competitive. In their report, the planners highlighted the car industry. They thought the Volga GAZ-24-10, powered by a V8 engine with 190 horsepower and heavily influenced by old Ford designs, could be an international winner. What a mistake!

The fact is that, after removing the barriers to international trade, all the socialist economies collapsed.[12] Most of them hit bottom about three to five years after the wall fell, with output falling around 40 percent. In some countries, like Poland, Hungary, and the Czech Republic, the output decrease was less dramatic—on the order of 15 to 20 percent. In other cases, like Georgia, Moldova, and the Ukraine, the economic collapse was even more severe; real output fell by 60 to 70 percent. By way of comparison, the US gross domestic product fell by about 30 percent between 1929 and 1933, during the Great Depression.

Estimating the impact of this output decline on the size of the Eastern European and Russian middle classes is difficult. Before 1989, Eastern Europeans and Soviets could not really be called members of the global middle class. They may have had some of the material aspects of a middle-class lifestyle, but they had none of the opportunities to represent themselves as a political class. Nor did they enjoy other traditionally middle-class choices of doing things or behaving in individualistic ways. Socialist countries were highly conformist countries. The diversity of goods that cater to individual tastes, so much a part of Western middle-class lifestyles, was absent in the Eastern Bloc.

After the change in political regimes, however, there was a huge rebound in economic fortunes and opportunities. Once stabilization had been achieved and structural reform began in the fifteen years after 1994, countries in Central and Eastern Europe and the former Soviet Union grew faster than at any time in the prior two hundred years and at two-and-a-half times the growth rate of their Western European counterparts.

From the perspective of the middle class, however, the crucial initial achievement was price stabilization. High inflation has long been the archenemy of the middle class. Across the Eastern Bloc in the early 1990s, inflation was a major factor, rising to more than 1,000 percent in seventeen out of twenty-five transition economies. Armenia, Georgia, Poland, and Ukraine suffered extensive hyperinflation. The first and most important economic policy reform, then, was to stabilize prices. The transition countries did this in different ways. Some, like Poland, fixed their currencies so that the price of imports would remain stable and act as a price anchor. Lithuania and Bulgaria did it by adopting a currency board, a legal arrangement that allowed central banks to print only as much money as the value of foreign exchange reserves in their coffers. Other countries adopted flexible exchange rates but took strong fiscal measures to limit government borrowing from the central bank. Within a few years, almost all former Eastern Bloc countries had brought inflation down to single-digit levels.

Along with stabilization, the transition economies moved quickly to reform their structures in other ways. An early move was small-scale privatization: changing ownership from the state to workers and managers of thousands of shops, garages, restaurants, hair salons, and other small-scale services. The emergence of individually owned small businesses through these privatization programs provided an immediate base for a new middle class.

The governance, restructuring, and sale of large enterprises kicked in a couple of years later, in parallel with reforms that liberalized the process of wage bargaining and of firm-level hiring and firing decisions. Although some firms became competitive through these measures, the number of employees in large enterprises dropped. Those lucky enough to keep their jobs could aspire to the middle class. For the others, it was a far harder road.

Central and Eastern European countries had a strange mixture of rapidly rising wage growth and rising unemployment. In East Germany, for example, one study finds that the average real wage of prime-age male workers rose by 83 percent in six years, even as the unemployment rate rose from 11 percent to 27 percent.[13] Among the European transition economies, even a decade after reforms, the average unemployment rate was in the double digits. An estimated 2.2 million people moved from Eastern European to Western European countries, not counting the large movements of East Germans to West Germany after reunification. Those who relocated found well-paying jobs that improved their own lives and were able to send billions of euros back home to their families.

The free movement of people within Europe was one of the great benefits of membership in the European Union, and much of the credit for the rapid improvement in the lives of people in Central and Eastern European countries goes to the willingness of the EU to expand its membership to the East. In 2004, the EU expanded by ten members, eight of which were transition economies (the others being Cyprus and Malta). Other countries were put on a path toward membership: Romania and Bulgaria joined in 2007, Croatia in 2013, and others are still in line. There was an immediate impact on migration. For example, by 2006, 5 percent of Poles had already emigrated to other European countries.

The EU has a distinctive cohesion policy that explicitly aims to reduce regional disparities in economic well-being and to generate economic dynamism and competitiveness in regions suffering from industrial and agricultural stagnation. Through regional funds (for local authorities and small business), social funds (for social protection and improving workforce skilling), cohesion funds (for poorer EU countries), and agricultural funds (for farmers), poorer regions in the EU receive money that can materially reduce inequality across the continent. The transition economies qualified for large portions of the EU funds.

Joining the EU is a complex process. Other member countries must be convinced that the newcomer has demonstrated a commitment to democracy, a market economy, and the rule of law to satisfy the criteria laid out by heads of state at a summit in Copenhagen, Denmark, in 1993. A unique feature of these criteria is the requirement for extensive legal rights governing social policy.

The free movement of labor is the most well-known of these rights, but the rules also govern contracts and workers' rights, antidiscrimination and fair treatment, health and safety at work, worker representation, information and consultation, redundancy policies, and works councils. In other words, many of the features that eased the entry of wage earners in Western Europe into the middle class were codified into laws and regulations that the newcomers had to adopt.

The Copenhagen criteria generated a convergence mechanism that allowed Central and Eastern European countries to bridge the economic gap with Western Europe in much the same way that Western Europe had converged with the United States after World War II. In another parallel, this convergence was also fueled by catch-up productivity growth in manufacturing and by the rapid expansion of trade. Within Europe, a new type of trade emerged. Rather than exchanging finished goods, trade was dominated by the exchange of intermediate goods within firms. For example, all the major automobile firms and their original equipment manufacturers (OEMs) established factories in Central and Eastern European countries, taking advantage of good infrastructure and well-developed supply chains.

An often-overlooked part of the economic benefits of EU integration is the political stability that came with it. The two-hundred-year-old struggle between capital and labor, which generated confidence-destroying swings in economic policies between populist and elitist governments in other parts of the world, was still being waged in Central and Eastern Europe, but the effects were tempered by the institutional guardrails put in place as a precondition of EU membership. Thanks to these institutions, the middle class has been able to take strong roots in both regions.

Billions of dollars flowed into Central and Eastern Europe, mostly driven by firms seeking the economic advantages of well-educated cheap labor, but a sizable portion also came from rich Western European governments. The West German government and private German firms, for example, poured about $2 trillion into East Germany in the three decades after reunification, more than $120,000 for every man, woman, and child in East Germany.[14] That translates into an amount roughly 250 times as large as what West Germany received through the Marshall Plan, even after adjusting for inflation between the two periods.

The figure is so large because of a fateful policy decision to unify the two economies in an arrangement that converted financial assets of the old East German mark into the West German deutsche mark at a rate of 1:1. All wages, salaries, rents, and pensions were converted at this rate. Savings accounts at banks were also converted at the same rate, although up to a ceiling that rose with the age of the holder. Other financial assets and loans were converted at the rate of 2 marks to 1 deutsche mark.[15] The policy reduced the gap in wages and wealth between the West and East but still left the East considerably poorer. What is more, banks and companies in the East could not compete with Western counterparts when they had to pay such high wages. Many of these firms were ultimately sold into private (largely West German) hands through a specially established agency, the Treuhandanstalt.

Other transition economies did not enjoy the same level of capital inflows as those going into East Germany, but the amounts were still substantial. The European Union's structural and cohesion funds were specifically designed to transfer resources from richer countries to poorer ones, and membership in the EU by itself was enough to reduce the cost of borrowing by sovereign governments—usually a good thing, but as Greece was to later discover when it overborrowed and had to make a massive correction, too much of a good thing is not always good.

The consequence of European convergence after the fall of the Berlin Wall was that almost the entire continent became predominantly middle class. Seventeen years after that fateful day in 1989, almost four out of every five households could be classified as middle class. Although households in Central and Eastern Europe remained far less well-off than those in Western Europe, regional disparities across the continent were no greater than in other large economies, like the United States. In a single generation, from 1975 to 2006, Europe's middle class had grown by 50 percent, with two hundred million more people among its ranks. More than 90 percent of the population in countries like Poland and Hungary could be counted in the middle class.

A Truly Global Middle Class Reaches Two Billion

The period of the Great Convergence, when the so-called second and third worlds started to catch up to the income levels of advanced economies, saw a rapid acceleration in the growth of the global middle class. It had taken 150 years for the first billion people to reach the middle class. It took only thirty-one years for another billion to join them, thanks to the power of the forces of globalization that were unleashed during the Great Convergence. By 2006, there were probably more than two billion people living in middle-class households around the world, and many of these were living in emerging and developing countries.

The way in which globalization affected the middle class differed by region. In East Asia, the main way was the opportunity to trade and continuously upgrade technology, oftentimes through copying what was happening in neighboring countries. East Asia had 485 million people in the global middle class in 2006.

In Latin America, globalization brought a new understanding of economic development—better ideas that allowed governments in the region to shed decades-old models of the role of the state and to converge on the idea of market-led economies with supportive, rather than extractive, public policies. Once economic stability was achieved, the natural resource wealth of these countries was able to support a large middle class. The region had around 290 million people in the middle class in 2006.

In Central and Eastern Europe, globalization facilitated the free movement of people and capital, underpinned by strong institutions guaranteeing rights for workers and for owners of private property. Accession to the EU, starting with interim agreements in 1994, marked the first time in history that laws and institutions were freely imported by countries as a package, in an effort to build prosperity fast. Previously, colonial powers or military victors had been able to impose their own laws on foreign subjects, but that was empire building, not middle-class building. The Europeans had 680 million people in the middle class in 2006.

At the beginning of the twenty-first century, then, the global middle class was larger and more geographically widespread than ever before. It had evolved through a greater variety of pathways. It was starting to morph into different variants, especially in Asia, but it still depended on the same fundamentals—education, good jobs, stable prices, and trust in a better future that encouraged thrift, hard work, and self-accountability.

Chapter 4

THE THIRD BILLION

China Dreams, but the West Is Alarmed, 2006–2014

> We must make persistent efforts, press ahead with indomitable will, continue to push forward the great cause of socialism with Chinese characteristics, and strive to achieve the Chinese dream of great rejuvenation of the Chinese nation.
>
> —Xi Jinping, 2012

In 2006, when the world's middle class had already surpassed two billion people, very few of them—almost surely less than 5 percent—lived in mainland China. The country had been growing rapidly for almost three decades since the start of economic reforms in 1979 and the introduction of the household responsibility system. Nevertheless, China's households were still poor and struggling, with only one-third of the country's national income going to private households for their own consumption.

Against this backdrop, the Sixteenth Central Committee of the Chinese Communist Party decided, in 2006 and 2007, to accelerate its efforts to build a "socialist harmonious society" to offset the social ills of growing income inequality and corruption that were accompanying unchecked economic growth. The vision of a harmonious society recalled ancient Chinese traditions of Confucianism and Taoism, or the way of nature. Translated for the modern world, achieving a harmonious society through "scientific development"—the means through which this new society would be attained—meant orienting government action toward reducing income inequalities, providing a well-founded rule of law perceived to be fair and just, and respecting nature. The concept of a harmonious society also signified an understanding that a more prosperous society would become more diverse, with multiple views and preferences among its population, and that there was more need for tolerance to resolve social friction in such a society.[1]

In brief, the Chinese Communist Party committed itself to building a domestic middle class, although it would never use such a term. The direction became clear in the twelfth Five-Year Plan, covering 2011–2016, when President Xi Jinping laid out his "Chinese dream" for the rejuvenation of the nation. No one quite knew the origin or the meaning of the Chinese dream nor whether it was a deliberate reference to the American dream or a throwback to ancient Chinese poetry. But when the most powerful man of the most populous country in the world talked, people listened.

Today, when the popular discussion about China revolves around when it will overtake the United States as the world's largest economy, it is easy to forget just how poor Chinese households were at the turn of the century. In 2000, the average person in a Chinese household in urban areas earned only about $760 a year. Two-thirds of the population was still rural, earning perhaps one-third of this amount. So only about 2 percent of the population, just over twenty million people, enjoyed middle-class lifestyles. In the ensuing decade, the middle class expanded, but the absolute numbers still remained low. At the start of the twelfth plan, fewer than one-quarter of Chinese households could afford what is commonly described as middle-class lifestyles.

The twelfth plan was framed at a time of one of the largest downturns in the global economy, caused by a banking and financial meltdown, first in the United States and then in Europe. This downturn, known as the Great Recession in the West and as the North Atlantic Financial Crisis in Asia, called for a change in policy direction in China's plan. Accordingly, the twelfth plan identified unsustainable elements in China's development as follows: an imbalanced dependence on investment and exports relative to domestic consumption; contradictions between economic growth and natural resources and the environment;

growing income disparities between rural and urban incomes; and growing social strife.

In short, China had to start developing its middle class to boost domestic demand to complement weaker prospects for international trade, and it had to do this without further polluting its air and the soil in which it grew its food. As is true with every issue linked to Chinese economics, the transition had to take place on a massive scale to have the desired effect. One of the most remarkable stories in the two centuries of middle-class expansion is how China, on its own, was able to add half a billion people to the ranks of the global middle class in just eight years, contributing about half of the increase in the middle class from two billion to three billion people between 2006 and 2014.

The rise of China's middle class coincided with a period when the middle class in the West was struggling to deal with the impact of recession, prompting an awkward question: Does the emergence of a large middle class in developing countries, including China, help or hurt the middle class in the West? Early thinking was that it would help; after all, the growth of the middle class in East Asia, Latin America, and Central and Eastern Europe had opened up trade opportunities and strengthened the middle class in the United States and Western Europe, so why wouldn't a larger middle class in China also help the Western middle class by providing new markets for exports and opportunities for cheap imports? The answer: It would bring sizable economic benefits but also costs, which are not evenly distributed. At the end of the twentieth century, it was believed that free trade would change China into a democratic country. President George H. W. Bush remarked in 1991 that "no nation on Earth has discovered a way to import the world's goods and services while stopping foreign ideas at the border."[2] Yet China has not moved toward greater democratization. If anything, a larger Chinese middle class has lent its support to the government, leaving the Communist Party even more firmly in control. The emerging Chinese middle class is different from that in the West. It has different views on individual liberties, responsibilities, and freedoms, especially when these conflict with collective actions for societal benefit. Think, for example, of the way in which China deployed a smartphone-based "health code" in response to the COVID-19 pandemic. This app allowed China to avoid a nationwide lockdown by a forced isolation of a targeted population once they were exposed to the virus, but it also used personal data and stringent government powers in a way that would likely not be acceptable in a Western democracy. Understanding these differences between the Chinese and Western middle classes is the first step in ensuring a peaceful coexistence and continued prosperity in East and West.

Building a Harmonious Middle-Class Society

The Chinese effort to construct a harmonious society started with urbanization, in much the same way as in Europe and the United States during the nineteenth century. Around 2000, China's urban population was large in absolute terms—around 450 million people—but it still represented only one-third of the total population of the country. Jobs and economic opportunities were concentrated in cities, especially in coastal areas, so large numbers of people moved there. On average, more than twenty million people each year have moved to cities in China since the turn of the twenty-first century. That is the equivalent of adding a new London and Paris combined every year. There are more than one hundred Chinese cities with more than one million people. The largest cities, Shanghai and Beijing, have twenty-seven million and twenty million inhabitants, respectively.

The rush to the cities created two big problems: how to find and create housing for everyone, and how to find and create jobs for everyone.

Until the 1990s, the building and maintenance of almost all urban housing was carried out by state-owned enterprises, and apartments were distributed by these enterprises to work units that in turn allocated them to families based on need, seniority, and marital status. A highly subsidized rent of 2 to 3 percent of wages was charged, but there was no incentive to provide decent housing, so apartments were small, overcrowded, and lacked interior showers and toilets.[3] Because rents were so low, the first efforts to sell housing to their occupants met with little success. Why buy when rents were so low? A gradual program of rent increases was set in motion, and gradually more people started to buy their accommodations. At the same time, private builders were encouraged to develop a private housing market. Because state-owned housing did not provide much space per person and was usually of low quality, the private developers focused on the top end of the market. This dual track of privatizing state-owned housing and encouraging the development of private housing markets led to a rapid expansion of home ownership to more than 80 percent of urban households by 2005.[4] By 1998, the State Council was able to completely abolish subsidized rentals provided by state-owned companies. What is more, almost all homes were owned outright, without mortgages, because the state-owned housing was sold off so cheaply.

This history meant that although Chinese households were poor when President Xi laid out his dream in 2012, one pillar of the middle class was already in place. The level of home ownership in urban areas was very high, indeed, far higher than in the United States, United Kingdom, or France, where home ownership is still less than two-thirds, and dramatically higher than in Germany, where only about half of all households own their residence. China fits the pattern of formerly socialist countries that all have very high rates of home ownership—Singapore is the only country in the top ranks of the global league table on home ownership rates that is neither socialist nor formerly socialist.

Despite rapid real estate development, prices for urban apartments in China are high and have grown rapidly for decades. This has been a boon to the existing middle class. Those who own an apartment (and many own two or more) have seen wealth accumulating at rates they could never achieve through their own labor earnings. For those who are entering the housing market, the up-front cost is high, but the financial returns are still huge. New migrants to cities and young households are often helped by family and friends to make a down payment. And because housing prices have systematically risen at a rate that far exceeds the interest rate on any money that has to be borrowed—the price per square meter doubled in the first decade of this century and has kept rising since—housing values have provided a solid foundation for building middle-class wealth in China.

Home ownership has been one way through which Chinese families have become rich enough to join the global middle class. It has also provided considerable psychological benefits. More living space adds to measures of self-reported satisfaction with life. When asked about which aspect of living conditions had most improved, many households mentioned the privacy and convenience offered by separate bedrooms and bathrooms for parents and children. Compared to renters, homeowners also have a reduced risk of being involuntarily moved and stay longer in a community. They build community ties with local businesses, get involved in local activities and management, and create stronger social networks with their neighbors. All these are aspects of the good life of a middle-class household.

The second great challenge in building the Chinese middle class was to generate enough good jobs. In 2006, the average annual household income per capita in China was only about $1,600, or roughly $5 per day.[5] Even adjusting for cost-of-living differences, this was just enough to bring a family to the bottom threshold of the global middle-class family. An added complication was that due to so much uncertainty over jobs and earnings, every household saved an average of one-quarter of their incomes every year, reducing the amount available to be spent on items like food, clothing, housing, transport, communication, education, and entertainment.[6]

With Chinese savings rates at such high levels—remember that US households have been saving only around 10 percent of their income over the last fifty years—the growth of the Chinese middle class depended heavily on generating more high-paying jobs. The old state-owned enterprises could not provide these. They were in fact shedding jobs to become more competitive in the face of an opening of the Chinese market to imports associated with China's entry into the World Trade Organization (WTO) in 2001. During the run-up to WTO entry between 1995 and 2002, state-owned enterprises shed more than thirty-six million jobs. Although they employed two out of every three urban workers in the late 1990s, by the time China actually joined the WTO, only one in two urban workers was employed by a state-owned enterprise.[7] Urban unemployment rose sharply, reaching double-digit levels (more than 11 percent) at the turn of the century.[8]

China is now known as the manufacturer for the world, but from a historical perspective, this is quite a recent phenomenon. When China joined the WTO, its exports of goods and services were about the same size as those from the Netherlands, a country with a population roughly one-hundredth that of China. During the next ten years, the value of China's exports grew more than sevenfold, and by 2012 China became the largest exporter in the world. Since 2006, it has employed more workers in manufacturing than the United States, France, Germany, Italy, Japan, Mexico, South Korea, and the United Kingdom combined.

At first, this boom in trade did not help develop China's middle class. True, a lot of jobs were created, but they were low paying. China had a deliberate policy of keeping wages low to encourage employment, and the sheer numbers of workers migrating from rural areas, about 135 million by 2007,[9] also allowed employers to keep wages low. Most of these migrant workers went to coastal cities with few legal protections or benefits. According to the US Bureau of Labor Statistics, the average hourly compensation of a Chinese worker in manufacturing in 2007 was about $1 per hour, a bit higher in cities and a bit lower in rural township and village enterprises. This was one-thirtieth the compensation level at the time for an average manufacturing worker in the United States and perhaps one-quarter to one-fifth the level of compensation in Mexico, Brazil, or Eastern Europe. It was nowhere close to the level needed to support a middle-class family—more than $30 per day for an average-sized family of three.

Not surprisingly, with wages at these levels, foreign investment into China boomed. Factories from all over the world were built in the Special Economic Zones set up in China's coastal provinces. These zones were industrial areas with all the required infrastructure—energy, water, transport to air- and seaports, and internet connectivity—and with business friendly regulations, such as duty-free imports and tax breaks. The largest boost to Chinese manufacturers, however, was not from domestic policy but from the termination of the international Agreement on Textiles and Clothing on January 1, 2005. The timing of this, coinciding with China's new strategy, was purely serendipitous. The seeds had been sown twenty years before, when China was a very minor player in the world of international trade and globalization.

Textiles and clothing had historically been excluded from international trade agreements because so many jobs depended on them, and they were deemed too sensitive to be subjected to global trade disciplines. For twenty years, from 1974 to 1994, international trade in textiles was governed by the "Multi Fibre Arrangement," which allowed countries to negotiate bilaterally with one another a set of restrictions on the quantity and tariff rates that were to be applied on imports of textiles and clothing. This system of individually negotiated deals undercut a core principle of the General Agreement on Tariffs and Trade, better known as the GATT, the organization that set global rules for trade. The very basis of the GATT was that all firms should be afforded the same opportunities regardless of their location. This is enshrined in its very first article on trade without discrimination, also known as the most-favored-nation clause. The GATT believed that all foreign members should be treated equally, and that national firms should be treated the same as foreign firms in each country's marketplace. When the GATT was formed, immediately after World War II, it was unrealistic to simply open up all markets instantaneously to free trade, so it managed a process of systematic trade liberalization among its major member economies.

By the mid-1980s, developing countries had become a far larger part of the global economy, but few were subject to the disciplines of the GATT. Quite the reverse. The GATT made considerable exceptions for developing countries, permitting them, through Article XVIII, to adopt quantitative restrictions and impose tariffs on imports in order to support infant industries and raise living standards. At the same time, new areas like intellectual property rights and trade in services were becoming important for advanced countries (financial services in particular were becoming more global and needed clear rules to operate in different jurisdictions). A deal was struck, starting with a conference held in Punta del Este, Uruguay, in 1986. Developing countries (excluding China, which was not an active member of the GATT at the time) would respect intellectual property rights and greater restrictions on their ability to impose trade, foreign ownership, and investment controls and regulations in the new areas of interest. In return, trade in textiles and clothing, where developing countries had a huge cost advantage, would be freed from the quantitative quotas and high tariffs being imposed by advanced countries.

The negotiations that followed, dubbed the Uruguay Round, took nine years to conclude. Among the agreements reached, two are central to our story. The Agreement on Textiles and Clothing replaced the Multi Fibre Arrangement and provided for a transition phase of ten years, after which all quotas and tariffs would be removed. This is why the market in these sectors suddenly opened up to free trade on January 1, 2005. It was significant because the production of garments and textiles is labor intensive and employs many women, permitting a large number of households to have two income earners.

The second major accomplishment of the Uruguay Round was an agreement to form the World Trade Organization, which started its operations on January 1, 1995. China wanted to be a founding member of the WTO, having gained observer status in the GATT in 1986, but, as a nonmarket economy, it had to implement significant internal reforms in order to be considered. These reforms included liberalizing services and regulations governing foreign investments in banking, finance, insurance, and telecommunications, and ending restrictions on wholesale, distribution, and retail trade. The conditions were substantially harsher than those applied to other developing countries, who have been allowed to keep many restrictions on their service sectors, but China was able to join the WTO on December 11, 2001, as a nonmarket economy. The implication of being a nonmarket member of the WTO is that other member states can more easily impose antidumping restrictions and tariffs on Chinese imports without China retaliating, a provision that has often been invoked in subsequent years.

For China, entry into the WTO offered important benefits. Before 2001, China had suffered from ad hoc trade restrictions that had been imposed on it for violating human rights, such as the Jackson-Vanik Amendment, which blocked normal trade and investment relations between China and the United States. President George H. W. Bush also used trade to punish China after the 1989 Tiananmen Square protests and massacre, and President Bill Clinton similarly linked China's most-favored-nation status renewal to conditions on human rights in Tibet.

After WTO entry, these restrictions were removed, and China gained normal trade relations with all WTO countries.

Most important, however, WTO membership signaled China's determination to move toward a market economy and to restrict state-owned enterprises to specific "commanding heights" of the economy. Most of China's exports consisted of office and telecommunications equipment and textiles and clothing manufactured by its newly dynamic private sector. Chinese entrepreneurs also were encouraged to join the Communist Party, a reversal of the ban that followed the Tiananmen protest about allowing "bourgeois" elements (code for businesspeople) into the party. It is not a coincidence that former president Jiang Zemin called for private businesspeople to join the Communist Party in his "Three Represents" speech in 2001, the same year that China joined the WTO.[10]

Bringing China into the WTO was (and remains) a controversial policy. True, Western consumers got cheap goods, and global inflation was kept low by China's ability to produce at scale. Western companies also saw higher profits by gaining access to Chinese markets and by offshoring their production to China to take advantage of cheap labor costs. US farmers saw exports of farm products to China rise fifteenfold, from $1.7 billion in 2001 to $26 billion in 2012. But workers in the manufacturing sector in Western countries, who opposed the agreement from the start, saw their employment and wages fall, largely due to automation but aggravated, in some cases, by globalization and trade.[11]

A quick aside: international trade is mutually beneficial when it takes place among economies that are operating at full employment. After China's entry into the WTO, unemployment in both the United States and Europe steadily fell for eight years. Encouraged by low inflation and low interest rates, Western economies shifted labor into higher value-added service sectors, prompting booms and bubbles in finance and real estate. When those bubbles burst, causing the Great Recession, the Western middle class was severely hit, and trade tensions with China have escalated ever since. Because of China's rise, large parts of the middle class in the West have abandoned their almost two-hundred-year stance in favor of free trade.

Returning to the story of China's growth: with trade providing opportunities to expand private business and with businesses getting political backing from the party, manufacturing production surged. It was easy for China to scale up production, as there was an almost unlimited supply of surplus labor coming to coastal cities from rural areas. Along with workers being shed from state-owned enterprises, it was not difficult to find a labor force willing to work for very low wages. This, however, had the effect of fostering extreme discontent among workers. Most Chinese urban workers belonged to a union, but the unions had little political power and never authorized strikes, so worker protests took the form of wildcat social disturbances. Dorothy Solinger, a professor of political science at the University of California, Irvine, cites the Ministry of Public Security as saying that "mass protests . . . began to rise like a violent wind" after 1997. She estimates that, during the decade before the turn of the century, there were one hundred thousand labor protests.[12]

Labor protests would continue, but on a diminished scale. They were largely left to municipal authorities to resolve, and, in truth, workers had very little political power. One of the key performance indicators for every Chinese local official was the ability to maintain tranquility, so local governments or companies wanting to curry favor with local officials made modest payments to workers to compensate for the perceived labor injustice; there was a premium on quickly resolving disputes. Municipalities were generating good money from the sale of land to property developers and could afford to offer compensation to those who lost their jobs. The system could not, however, be sustained, and in 2008, the central government introduced several new pieces of legislation to strengthen workers' rights: a Labor Contract Law, an Employment Promotion Law, and a Labor Dispute Mediation and Arbitration Law.[13]

Around this time, labor shortages also started to occur in some segments of the workforce. The municipal government of Shenzhen, home to China's first Special Economic Zone, negotiated a collective bargaining agreement with workers in the zone. In a famous episode in 2010, workers at a Honda plant in Guangdong went on strike and won wage increases that almost doubled the wage rate for some workers. That same year, a Shenzhen plant of the electronics giant Foxconn, famous for its production of iPhones, doubled its wage rates after fifteen suicide attempts by workers throwing themselves off the roof of the factory building, mostly with fatal results.[14]

By 2014, China's average wage in manufacturing had risen to $8,400 per year, more than enough to provide a basic middle-class living standard for a small family. The trajectory of wage increases would continue steadily upward, and in 2019 it had surpassed $11,000. With unemployment hovering around 4 percent and more than half the total population employed, China was well on its way to becoming a middle-class economy.

No story of China's move toward a middle-class society would be complete without considering the impact of education, which later would be reflected in higher productivity and better wages for new job entrants. The important role of education in forming the middle class in high-performing Asian economies was already noted in the last chapter. China would replicate this experience on a scale that had never before been seen. Deng Xiaoping restored China's National Higher Education Entrance Exam in 1977 as a meritocratic system for accepting students into university—a break from the Maoist system of sending the intellectual students into the countryside rather than to university while reserving university placement for those with the right political and class backgrounds. But it took some time to build the system. In 1999, the central government decided to expand the scale of higher education. Between 1999 and 2020, the number of higher education institutions in China increased from roughly one thousand to three thousand, allowing enrollment to grow from one-and-a-half million to eight million students each year, about 40 percent of the eighteen-year-old cohort. There is still a long way to go. By comparison, more than two-thirds of US students go on to either a two-year or a four-year college.

Quality increased along with quantity of education. In 2009, the Shanghai Municipal Education Commission asked the Organization for Economic Cooperation and Development, a club of advanced economies, to include Shanghai in an international standardized test of fifteen-year-olds on reading, mathematics, and science proficiency that the organization undertakes every three years. The Programme for International Student Assessment (PISA), as the test is known, seeks to monitor whether students will be able to apply the knowledge learned in school to real-world concerns. It is a comparative learning exercise to identify the efficiency and effectiveness of different systems, and it therefore focuses on average scores and the scores of the most disadvantaged students. When Shanghai was included, it came out with the best average scores in the world, as well as the lowest share of low achievers.[15]

Shanghai is, of course, not representative of China, and a single test does not provide a good data point, but the test has now been repeated four times, each time with outstanding results for China. In the most recent round in 2018, Beijing, Jiangsu, and Zhejiang joined Shanghai in the assessment and again the average score was the best of any country in the world. The four provinces combined have a population of 180 million people, so although still not representative of China, they account for a substantial number of households. Of course, there are large variations within China on educational attainment, with poorer provinces and regions such as Tibet performing at a far lower level. In fact, in the 2015 PISA exercise, Guangdong province was included and led to a far lower average result for China as a whole, dropping China from first place. Nevertheless, the achievement of reaching the top ranks in education in the world is noteworthy.

Education is not simply a tap that can be turned on to create a growing economy and middle class. Jobs must be provided at the same time. China, like many other countries, has wrestled with an oversupply of university graduates at times. But the expanding base of schooling has helped improve this situation. More and better schools require more and better teachers, and China has developed a culture in which teachers enjoy high social status; many of the best students choose to enter teaching as a profession. At the same time, students see the economic benefits of higher education and strive for excellence in school. Chinese high school students put in more hours of work every day, in addition to the standard thirty-hour school week, than in any other country. This is not all positive from the standpoint of the individual—the stress on students is immense—but it does generate a highly competitive and efficient system of learning.

This feedback loop between the education system and social status is a noteworthy feature of the middle class in China and many other Asian countries. It is not just a matter of doing well on exams by remembering facts and figures. Instead, the education system tries to embed values and cooperation, communication, creativity, and social interaction skills. The competition induced by test taking is merely an incentive to improve. In China, it is also an instrument for social change and progress. Want to reduce the level of child obesity, which has now reached one in five children? Make physical exercise part of the core test (scored equally with Chinese language proficiency). Want to build creativity and innovative thinking? Build arts and music into the test. With innovations like these and a focus on professional development of teachers and parent training (a lot of learning gets done at home), the challenge of creating an education system that can deliver qualified workers for an expanding middle class can be met.[16]

Nonmonetary Issues Affecting the Middle Class: Pollution and Food Safety

It is easy to overestimate China's progress in developing a middle class by looking only at material consumption and ignoring the nonmonetary issues that are also important for the middle class. Recall that material consumption might be a convenient way of measuring the middle class, but it is only a proxy for a much broader concept of the ability to live a good life. The Chinese government would have to deal with these other issues as well before it could lay claim to being a champion of the middle class.

In January 2013, just a few months after Xi Jinping's "Chinese dream" speech, Beijing experienced what residents called an "airpocalypse," a level of particulates in the air that was 4,000 percent higher than the level deemed safe for humans to breathe by the World Health Organization. A couple years later, in December 2015, Beijing's municipal government felt compelled to close schools, restrict traffic, and reduce factory and construction activities in the face of another great smog.

The increase in pollution alongside economic growth and a larger middle class was not unique to China's experience. London suffered from a Great Smog in 1952, caused, as in Beijing, by burning large amounts of coal during the depths of winter at a time when wind conditions stopped the particulates from blowing away. In both instances, a warm "lid" of air sat on top of the city in what is called a temperature inversion, trapping and accumulating ever more particulates from the burning of fossil fuels. Factories and car exhaust added to the problem. In London, as many as ten thousand people died as a result of the Great Smog, mostly among those with preexisting respiratory problems, and probably another one hundred thousand people were sickened. There are no comparable numbers for Beijing, but millions of people throughout China's northern belt were affected. Visibility was so poor that only ten stories of high-rise buildings could be seen from the ground. According to some stories, even buses found themselves lost on the road.

China's leadership recognized that pollution was an existential threat to the Chinese dream. Premier Li Keqiang vowed to upgrade development so that "people can enjoy clean air and safe drinking water and food."[17] He promised to use an iron fist to tackle the problems.

In September 2013, the government unveiled a five-year plan aimed squarely at pollution: the Airborne Pollution and Prevention Action Plan, 2013–2017. The plan set goals to reduce the level of particulates in northern provinces and cities by 15 to 25 percent and provided funding from the central government to replace coal-fired boilers and other polluting machinery. Individual cities and provinces set up their own plans; local officials were made accountable for the results.

The results were tangible. Over the plan period, the pollution levels faced by the average person in the affected regions fell by about one-third, largely by strengthening emissions standards, upgrading industrial equipment (especially in steel plants), and promoting clean fuels in the residential sector.[18] But the problem was not nearly solved. In early 2015, Chai Jing, an investigative reporter and former TV host, made a documentary called *Under the Dome*. Poignantly starting with her own pregnancy and her fears for her daughter, Chai summarizes the hopes of a Chinese middle-class mother: "My only wish was for my family to stay healthy and to be together."[19] For almost two hours, the video records the problems in China, from energy dependence on coal, to subsidies for energy-dependent heavy industry, to the monopoly of PetroChina restricting natural gas production, to enforcement problems with small leakages from restaurants, gas pumps, and other everyday aspects of fossil-fuel consumption. It was viewed in China by two hundred million people before being censored.

PM2.5, the concentration in the air of particulate matter of less than 2.5 micrometers (about one-tenth the diameter of the finest human hair), is now a familiar concept in every household in China, as regularly monitored on smartphones as the weather. It may have become a more politically salient metric than even gross domestic product (GDP) or household income growth. The tiny particles monitored by PM2.5 penetrate deep into the lungs, and even into the bloodstream, causing cancers, respiratory disease, and heart attacks. They are less tangible than the larger PM10 particles that are linked to sore throats, coughing, and irritation of the eyes and nose but more deadly to humans.

China has made noteworthy strides in improving air quality, but the number of deaths from air pollution, even adjusted for population size, is still three to four times higher than in countries with comparable income levels, such as Brazil, Mexico, Colombia, or Thailand. And advanced economies such as the United States and Spain have one-tenth the per capita deaths from air pollution as China, so there is a long way to go.

The start, and where China has made most progress, is actually in addressing indoor air pollution. It is common in developing countries for poor households to cook over an open fire or on stoves with poor ventilation, usually using coal, wood, and animal dung and crop waste in rural areas. The smoke inhalation is dangerous, as there are multiple types of particles due to incomplete combustion. Women who spend considerable time in the kitchen areas preparing food are particularly at risk, and pregnant women can have complications such as stillbirths or low-weight births associated with indoor air pollution.

Around 2000, three-quarters of all Chinese households were exposed to indoor air pollution from the burning of solid fuels. That level has been cut in half thanks to urbanization and improved living standards. Almost all middle-class households now have clean electric or gas stoves. In 2017, the government tried to force through a rapid replacement of coal-burning heaters but with limited success. Natural gas was in short supply. Reports of schoolchildren attending class outside in winter because old heaters had been removed before new heaters were provided attracted national attention and led to the programs being scaled back and reversed in some places.

China has recently announced more ambitious national commitments under the Paris Climate Agreement, setting itself targets of net zero carbon emissions by 2060 and of peak emissions before 2030. It has launched a nationwide carbon trading market. In 2021 the scheme was focused on the two thousand power plants that supply electricity in China, but it will later be extended to heavy industries like steel, cement, aluminum, chemicals, and petroleum production and refining. Doubtless, China is keen to contribute to saving the planet, but the real pressure comes from China's own middle class. Young people are eager to take part, and new university programs in clean energy have become popular majors.

In most advanced countries, societal interests on issues like the environment have been supported by a well-developed system of nongovernmental organizations (NGOs). Such organizations are critical channels for furthering the class interests of poor, middle class, or even rich households. In China, one of the first successful suits brought by an environmental group against a company was the Nanping case in 2015. A local company in Fujian province had illegally quarried stone and dumped waste materials while building roads through protected forests. Despite a cease-and-desist order from the local ministry, the company continued these practices. A local court found the owners guilty of appropriating agricultural and forest land and sentenced them to prison. After a subsequent court case, the company was forced to pay damages and to restore the forest to its original state.[20]

China does not have a well-developed NGO sector. The number of NGOs is only about seven hundred in a country of 1.3 billion people, so the ability of the middle class to exercise its political muscle to push for more rapid change is weak. (For comparison, the United States has about fifteen thousand registered environment and nature

NGOs.) Chinese NGOs generally limit themselves to filing suit against companies rather than against government agencies. For that, state prosecutorial organs are used. In 2018 alone, some fifty-five thousand environmental cases were filed by state prosecutors representing public interest legal challenges on environmental issues.

The middle-class pressure to control pollution in China was matched by pressure to enjoy safe food. After all, food still comprises one-third of Chinese middle-class expenditures. As Chinese households moved out of rural areas into cities and started to enjoy middle-class lifestyles, they also altered their diets to include processed food. A very large number of food production facilities with long value chains from farm to table were needed to satisfy urban consumers' demand for food. In the process, biotoxins, heavy metals, and microorganisms entered the food supply. Fertilizers and pesticides were heavily overused. In one infamous case in 2011, a local pig farm supplying one of China's largest meat distributors was found to be using a medication named clenbuterol. Clenbuterol is approved for use only in horses in the United States because of its cardiovascular and neurological side effects in humans, and it was also banned in China but nevertheless illegally used by some companies.

The process of establishing sound food safety is complicated, with many incentives for companies to cheat in the interest of making more money. China has had a Food Safety Law since 2009, and in 2017 the Nineteenth Congress of the Communist Party introduced the concept of "Healthy China" into its program. But control is hard. A major problem is the overuse of illegal food additives: preservatives and stabilizers to extend product shelf life, sweeteners to improve taste, and colorants to make food look more appetizing.[21] Carcinogenic red dye has been found in chicken products; cadmium from industrial contamination in Chinese rice is the highest in the world; melamine, which can cause kidney failure, has been added to watered-down milk to help it pass quality control tests. The 2008 melamine scandal reportedly caused the hospitalization of fifty-three thousand babies.[22]

Following a revised Food Safety Law in 2015, China began to strengthen the role of social groups in food safety. The China Consumers Association now tests products, issues consumer warnings, and responds to consumer queries. Internet-based social media, such as Weibo and WeChat, provide platforms for reports on food safety issues.

The Chinese middle class is trying to flex its muscle and force the government to act on both pollution and food safety issues. Given China's political system, the way in which the middle class influences government policy is quite different compared to other countries. In democracies, the middle class can force a change of government by voting for one party instead of another, and it organizes advocacy NGO groups to advance its interests. In China, the middle class tries to achieve change by the sheer weight of numbers and public opinion. Organized voices of the middle class, be they unions or NGOs, are not particularly powerful or influential in opposing the state. But, as discussed later, the power of the people's voice can be expressed in other ways, especially in a digital age.

China does not yet enjoy many of the safeguards of clean air and water and safe food and drugs, which would typically be expected by the middle class. In many ways, it has grown more rapidly than the institutions that deliver these safeguards. As a consequence, indicators of material well-being probably overstate the degree of actual progress in overall well-being. Nevertheless, it seems clear that the speed of China's middle-class growth has been unprecedented. In 2006, only 7 percent of China's population could be considered middle-class by global standards. Eight years later, by 2014, more than 40 percent of the population lived in a middle-class household. For comparison, the United States took seventy-five years to make this same progression, from 1830 to 1905. China accounted for half of the additional one billion middle-class people added between 2006 and 2014.

Alarm in the Western Middle Class

When the world's middle class increased from two billion to three billion people between 2006 and 2014, just under half the new middle-class households were in China. During this period, the most well-established part of the global middle class, in America and Europe, was experiencing its most sustained difficulties in a century and a half. It is tempting to draw a causal connection between the two, to argue that the expansion of Chinese and other Asian households into the middle class came at the expense of those in the West, but this is incorrect. The structural stresses on parts of the middle class in America—for example, those causing white males to drop out of the labor force—clearly started before China's entry into the WTO and the rapid expansion of Chinese exports. And the financial weaknesses and policy mistakes in Europe in dealing with its own financial crisis are unrelated to what was happening in Asia.

Following the Great Recession in 2009, North America and Western Europe suffered the worst downturn in their economies since the Great Depression. Along with this came a dramatic change in the size and structure of the Western middle class. Because the two trends—a rising Chinese middle class along with a shrinking, or at least suffering, Western middle class—took place at the same time, there was inevitable discussion and analysis as to whether the good fortune of China was causing the misfortunes in the West.

The arguments about the causal relationships in comparative cross-country economic performance have a long history. Over a century ago, in 1903, John Maynard Keynes, then an undergraduate at Cambridge University, gave a speech on the "spirit of nationalism," which he described as a feeling that anyone else's prosperity is damaging to you, that nationalism conveyed a feeling of jealousy and hatred. Based on this, Keynes argued that nationalism was one of the greatest obstacles to the progress of civilization because of the us-versus-them mentality it created. His bolder vision was that if there was sufficient prosperity everywhere, then people would be satisfied with enough material goods, and there would be little need to resort to war between nations in an effort to capture more resources. Countries and social classes would instead argue about ideas and philosophies. This was the basis for his strong support of free trade, a policy that he believed would lead to prosperity for both exporter and importer.

Keynes's vision of the power of free trade in bringing nations together was a staple of international politics throughout the twentieth century. It was the basis for the formation of the 1951 Treaty of Paris, an agreement among six formerly warring European states to form an integrated coal and steel community for the efficient reconstruction of

Europe. This treaty went on to be expanded into the European Union. Free trade and mutual prosperity have also been the basis of stability among the highly diverse Muslim, Hindu, Buddhist, and Christian countries in the Association of Southeast Asian Nations.

It remains to be seen whether economic and financial links between China and the West will be strong enough to avert armed conflict between them, and much depends on whether trade with China is seen as a net positive for Western economies. One line of thinking is that it has cost jobs, although US manufacturing jobs declined well before trade with China grew large. US employment had already successfully transitioned from manufacturing to services without any increase in unemployment before 2001, the year that China joined the WTO. In January 2001, the unemployment rate was just 4 percent, the lowest level in more than thirty years, and three-quarters of workers were employed in the services sector, including finance and real estate. Then job growth slowed to less than 1 percent per year, the economy became ever more dependent on credit, the stock market began to wobble, and housing prices fell. In 2007 two sizable mortgage lenders went bankrupt, followed in 2008 by the managed acquisition of Bear Stearns by JPMorgan Chase and, on September 15, by the bankruptcy of Lehman Brothers, the fourth largest US investment bank. On September 16, 2008, the Dow Jones index fell by more than 500 points.

The Great Recession was devastating for the middle class in the West. It savaged wealth. American households and nonprofits lost $14 trillion in their net worth during the course of the Great Recession. It destroyed jobs; from 2007 to 2010, the United States lost ten million jobs and the unemployment rate climbed to almost 10 percent. One-fourth of American households were "under water" on their mortgages—that is, they owed more than the value of their house.

Beyond the aggregates, the impact of the Great Recession on different parts of the American middle class was quite varied. Places with weak economies, such as some rural areas and poorer suburban areas with large minority communities, were especially hard hit. Making matters worse, there was a snowball effect, afflicting entire neighborhoods. Banks were unwilling to lend to places with large numbers of foreclosed houses, which drove prices down even further in those locations. And as people abandoned or were evicted from their houses, maintenance fell and neighborhood crime rates rose.

The economic shock of the Great Recession was especially difficult for groups that were already suffering. Starting in 1998, one of the longest trends in American well-being, the improvement of life expectancy and fall in morbidity, reversed itself for white, noncollege-educated prime working age males in America. In a seminal study looking at the change in reported well-being between a starting period of 1997 to 1999 and an end period of 2011 to 2013, Princeton economists Anne Case and Angus Deaton shocked the profession by reporting that deaths from drug and alcohol poisonings, suicides, and chronic liver disease—deaths of despair—had shot up for some White male groups by so much that life expectancy was starting to fall.[23] This was not a generalized phenomenon, and the finding came as a surprise. It was not seen in other advanced economies, nor among Black or Hispanic populations within the United States. It was not true for college-educated males. It was very specific to the group of white males with high school education or less.

In addition to higher mortality, the group of noncollege-educated white males reported more days of poor physical and mental health. They complained that they had to limit their daily activities because of physical or mental pain. They consumed more alcohol. There was a large increase in the number leaving the workforce and receiving disability insurance payments. Their symptoms resulted in opioid prescriptions becoming more widely available beginning in the late 1990s.

The year 2000 also marked the entry of the first millennials into the labor force. Millennials faced a radically different economic environment compared to their parents. Whereas 90 percent of children born in the 1950s enjoyed a higher living standard than their parents, the same was true for only 50 percent of those born after 1980.[24]

It is not clear exactly what caused that, but it seems clear that stresses in the US middle class predate the emergence of a large Chinese middle class. The last twenty years has seen a considerable fall in social mobility in the United States. Children raised in poor households had limited chances of improving their own lot in life. This was so contrary to the spirit of the American dream, to the narrative that hard work and a good education would be the ticket to success, that it also became linked to a decline in optimism and hope for the future. White American noncollege-educated males started to drop out of the labor force, to be less optimistic about their future, and to stay in a disgruntled state in their home environments. Geographic mobility declined at the same time as social mobility.[25]

The cleavage in the American middle class in this century is stark. College-educated people are still, in general, optimistic and believe that life offers them many opportunities. Many of those without a college education, however, have become pessimists, living at home, unable or unwilling to move, either physically or mentally, as the economic environment shifts. Part of this may be due to competition with China and the decline in manufacturing jobs in America more broadly. But those structural trends affected all groups, whereas the drop in optimism and mobility is concentrated among men rather than women, among whites rather than Blacks or Hispanics, and among prime age males rather than the young and the old. It would seem that deeper cultural forces are at play, as well as the superficial changes in economic structure.

The Great Recession, then, accentuated the split within the American middle class that was already starting in 1998, several years before China joined the WTO, and that seems to be related to automation. The generation that thought they could comfortably continue with middle-class lifestyles, like their parents before them, without having to go on to college, was severely disappointed when it lost its old jobs and found it lacked the skills to get good new jobs in other sectors. Many millennials found out too late how bad their educational choices had been. When the Great Recession wiped out this generation's savings and their jobs, there was little it could do to respond.

This group slowly started slipping out of the middle class into relative poverty. At the same time, the Great Recession meant that previously rich households returned to the middle class, albeit temporarily. As the latter group of households later enjoyed the benefits of a recovering labor market, a more profitable environment for the small businesses that many owned or were starting, and a soaring stock market, they regained their wealth. So the middle class in America started to shrink—the richer members became rich, while the least well-off members fell back into near poverty. By 2014, when the three billionth person joined the global middle class, the size of the American middle class already was falling in absolute numbers, and the middle class was becoming divided. The gap widened between those who had a college education (and could participate in the new digital economy) and those who did not. Rather than having common cause on economic issues, these different segments of the middle class now have different economic priorities.

Europe too was having economic problems at this time. The subprime mortgages that had sunk US banks had also been sold to European banks. These banks were the financial lifelines for many governments at the time. When the banks lost money, they had to pull back on their sovereign loans. Governments in Ireland, Portugal, Greece, and Cyprus found that they could not refinance their debts. They needed new loans, which they were able to get from the International Monetary Fund and from the European Union. But these loans had strong conditions attached to them. Governments had to cut spending, including on pensions, public wages, and other social transfers. The economies went into a tailspin. Greece, for example, had a negative per capita economic growth rate for six successive years. At its worst point, the average Greek income was less than three-quarters the level of its peak in 2007. It took the United States two years to recover from the Great Recession. Greece will be lucky if it returns to its 2008 income level in twenty-five years.

The period after the Great Recession saw the center of gravity of the global economy shift rapidly toward Asia. Imagine a globe that is cut up, flattened into two dimensions, and gridded into 710 areas. Put a weight on each area proportional to the output produced in that area, then find the center of gravity of the resulting model, the spot where it is exactly in balance. This is what economist Danny Quah has done.[26] He shows that in 1980 the earth's economic center of gravity was somewhere in the mid-Atlantic, reflecting the weight of production in North America on the one hand and Europe on the other hand. But by 2014, the center of gravity had shifted to a spot somewhere in Iran. It had moved due east. That is why in 2014, when the global middle class reached three billion, there were more middle-class people living in developing countries than in the advanced countries of the world, and why just shy of four out of every five members of the third billion members of the global middle class lived in Asia.

~

Chapter 5

THE FOURTH BILLION

The Indian Elephant in the Room, 2013–2021

No power on earth can stop an idea whose time has come.

—Victor Hugo, quoted in 1991 by then
Indian Finance Minister Manmohan Singh
in his budget speech to Parliament

Prime Minister Manmohan Singh, first elected in 2004, was widely acknowledged as the architect of India's economic reforms. Singh's big idea was that the government in India was part of the problem rather than the solution for India's economic development. His reform programs were designed to unleash entrepreneurship and private business initiative in India, to underline the individual's responsibility for his or her family's prosperity. It was a classic middle-class agenda. From an economic point of view, his efforts were spectacularly successful. From a political point of view, they were not. In 2014, Singh was forced to step down from office after his Congress Party was roundly defeated at the polls by the Bharatiya Janata Party (BJP), which captured the imagination of the Indian middle class.

The foundations of India's modern economic development were laid in 1991, when Singh was appointed India's finance minister, the first political job for someone who had until then had a distinguished career as a technocrat. At that time, India was on the verge of crisis: its foreign exchange reserves had shrunk to perhaps two weeks of imports, and the country faced a large external financing gap that no foreign lenders were prepared to fill. Years of operating the economy under a

License Raj, a system that required permits (typically multiple permits) from the government to engage in almost any form of economic activity, had suffocated initiative and entrepreneurship and left hundreds of millions of households in extreme poverty.

Fortunately for Singh, he was not alone in his desire to dismantle the permit raj. Two years before, liberalizers in the Ministry of Industry had begun to draw up a plan to decontrol industry, invite foreign investments, and open up to foreign technologies. The plan went nowhere, as the government of V. P. Singh (no relation) faced internal political rebellion and collapsed, but the planning had been done. So when the new finance minister wanted a set of bold actions, he did not need to speak in generalities; he could be quite specific and detailed and confident about the technical soundness of the reforms he was about to champion.

Singh used to compare India's Hindustan Motors with Toyota as a way of conveying the stultification that had befallen Indian industry. Hindustan Motors started its operations in 1942, just five years after Toyota. It had all the advantages of a large and captive domestic market in which it was able to win a 75 percent market share at its peak. Its initial design of its iconic Ambassador model was based on the successful Morris Oxford Series III. Well suited to domestic conditions, with the roominess and sturdiness required for journeys on India's potholed and often unpaved roads, the Ambassador was the car of choice for India's government officials.

The problem was that lack of competition in Indian industry led to lack of ambition. Hindustan Motors put no money into research and development or branding and advertising. In the early 1990s, the capacity at its west Bengal plant was only twenty-five thousand cars per year. In 1991, Toyota, a company that set out to be a global leader from the time of its founding, produced four million passenger cars and light trucks annually, and its Lexus was the top-selling premium car import in the United States, with the highest quality ranking in the J. D. Power surveys of vehicle quality and consumer satisfaction. By comparing Hindustan Motors with Toyota, Singh understood that India could not create a world-class manufacturing sector that would generate the jobs to support a large middle class, as had happened in other countries, without a new policy approach that would create globally competitive businesses.

He decided to act. In an ironic twist of history, the plan for Indian economic revival came out of the Ministry of Industry, but the driver of Indian economic growth that was to follow was the development of the services sector. India stands alone among countries in building its middle class through the massive expansion of its service occupations rather than through manufacturing. As the actor Shekhar Kapur would say: "It was expected of all good middle-class Indian people to build India and, as you know, Indians—when we say, 'build India,' it was all about being an accountant, a lawyer, an engineer. So, it was this idea that professionals would build the country."

It was only the engineers who were able to scale their contributions, using the new technologies of the global economy that were creating opportunities that had never existed before. After the internet developed into a global commercial network in the 1990s, software engineers became the springboard for Indian prosperity. The Indian middle class saw an astonishing growth from 2013 to 2021. In 2013, only about one in six Indians could be considered as being in the global middle class. These were salaried employees, many in the civil service who enjoyed considerable perks even if they had modest incomes. There were also the professionals—doctors, lawyers, bankers—whose income levels afforded them a good lifestyle given the low prices in India. By 2021, however, as India recovered from the setback associated with the global COVID-19 pandemic, this core middle class had more than doubled in size, adding three hundred million people. The growth of the Indian economy during this period created small businesses and a demand for teachers, nurses in private clinics and schools, bank tellers and tradesmen everywhere, and mechanics and developers of the new "census towns," peri-urban areas into which rural Indians migrated. Indians were the largest source of the new middle class in the world during this period. The accomplishment is all the more remarkable because it includes the 2020 recession, the country's deepest and widest economic contraction in modern times, when India's output fell by an estimated 7 percent.

Service with a Smile: The Emergence of an Indian Middle Class

Software is the heart and soul of India's services sector and the engine of economic growth in the country. Tata Consultancy Services (TCS), Infosys, and Wipro are leading global brands, and TCS has moved in and out of the top spot in the rankings of the world's most valuable information technology (IT) companies. As with many great companies, luck played a major part in the story. India happened to have the human talent required, thanks to institutions that had been set up shortly after independence in 1947. It also happened to have deregulated its telecommunications sector earlier than many other countries because the state-owned phone monopoly was so bad that it had few friends. Everyone supported the idea of doing something to improve telecommunication services. Thanks to those reforms, India has now become one of the cheapest places in the world to have an internet connection or broadband package, so it is well placed to use the latest general-purpose technologies of the digital revolution.

The foundation of India's software industry is unquestionably India's large and growing pool of skilled engineers. Starting in 1951, India committed itself to building Indian Institutes of Technology (IIT), taking inspiration from the Massachusetts Institute of Technology. The first such institute was built over a prison camp at Kharagpur, where the British had held Indians fighting for independence. Prime Minister Jawaharlal Nehru, in addressing the assembly at IIT Kharagpur in 1956, said: "Here in the place of that Hijli Detention Camp stands the fine monument of India, representing India's urges, India's future in the making. This picture seems to me symbolic of the changes that are coming to India."[1] Not even Nehru could have imagined the changes that his IITs would bring to India, nor that it would take a full fifty years before the potential of the IITs to drive Indian economic development would be fully realized.

Through the 1990s, many of the IIT graduates ended up in America and the United Kingdom, having gone abroad for graduate work, postdoctoral studies, or a job opportunity. Among these was Vinod Khosla, founder of Sun Microsystems, a graduate of IIT Delhi, who would credit his success to the intense competition of getting into and then succeeding in an IIT school. But as India began to liberalize, the diaspora started to return, and new graduates found opportunities in India. The core of engineers who could supply the software demanded by the world was in place.

The second part of India's software success was its excellent communications with the rest of the world. In the 1990s, when Manmohan Singh's reforms started, India was a poor country, so in many ways it is strange that it became so successful in a high-tech industry like IT. Its economic backwardness proved to be its critical strength, however. When the political decision to de-bureaucratize the country was taken in 1991, there were only five million telephones in all of India, a country which then had a population of 890 million people. In the previous decade, only three million phones had been added while the population had grown by 180 million. At these rates, India was rapidly moving backward in the percentage of households with access to a phone. The state-owned Department of Telecom had a monopoly over telephone services. And it did what all monopolies are prone to do: restrict supply and charge high prices, especially for the lucrative long-distance phone service.

As part of Finance Minister Singh's drive to reduce the public sector's presence in the Indian economy, the government passed a National Telecommunications Policy in 1994, auctioning off licenses to operate mobile services and basic phone services in eighteen to twenty different domestic geographies where a private company could compete with the state-owned company. Foreigners were allowed to own a minority share. In 1997, a new Telecom Regulatory Authority of India opened more space for private-sector initiatives on pricing and other areas. A series of amendments and other policy changes steadily reduced government engagement and opened the sector to foreign and domestic investors. The volume and value of mobile phone services exploded, connecting India with the rest of the world.

So by the 2000s, India had in place two critical foundations for successful development of its software industry. It had skilled, cheap talent, and it had the ability to cheaply export data and code anywhere in the world from almost anywhere in the country.

At this time during the early 2000s, a starting Indian software engineer was paid a salary of 2.5 to 3 lakhs of rupees, around $10,000 per year. An equivalent engineer in the United States was making $70,000 and up to $100,000, including year-end bonuses.[2] With wage differentials of 10:1, it is not surprising that investors poured money into India. By 2013, India had about 2.75 million software engineers, a number that was roughly doubling every five years, according to Evans Data Corporation, a global market intelligence firm in the software business. Each engineer probably indirectly supported three additional jobs in the sectors using their services. These engineers could work all over India, although they were concentrated in a few IT hubs.

India had 3.5 million cell phone subscribers in 2000, 750 million in 2010, and one billion by 2015.[3] Of these, there were about 239 million smartphone users in 2015, surpassing the number in the United States. India had some of the lowest rates per call in the world, thanks to cutthroat competition among providers. It had 140 million broadband subscribers.[4]

The combination proved powerful. In the early days, before the internet was widely used commercially, Indian software firms had been able to provide customized solutions to companies starting to computerize their operations. Coding for services like financial funds transfer and accounting had to be done separately for each hardware system. Indian firms found that the easiest solution was to "body shop." They sent their engineers abroad to sit with clients, do the work, and then come home. It was a transactional business, hard to scale. There were expensive losses when engineers were poached by foreign firms and their replacements had to be trained. Most of the client demand was for routine tasks with low profit margins, so although there was growth, the money involved was not large enough to be transformative in a country as large as India.

Once the internet was in place, however, starting after the Y2K scare—which gave Indian companies considerable international exposure as problem solvers—global multinationals invested in research and development and business process management centers in India. Physically concentrated in a few cities, these centers have evolved into a full-blown software ecosystem of multiple clients, providers, innovators, and new tech entrepreneurs with revenues doubling every five years.

So it was that in 2015, India's export revenue from the IT sector was $100 billion. The number of local tech start-ups was doubling every five years. Some served export markets, but a growing number served India's domestic market, cashing in on the demands and habits of the new Indian middle class.[5] Flipkart, the Indian version of Amazon, was valued in early 2021 at $25 billion. A slew of other unicorns, firms valued at over $1 billion, followed.

Every successful economy needs a few sectors where it is dominant in international markets. Germany is famous for chemicals and automobiles; Japan dominates consumer electronics; China leads in clothing, computers, and anything made of plastic. Information technology plays this role in India. It accounts for one-quarter of India's exports and one-twelfth of its total output. It is driving education. The software industry collaborative FutureSkills program has a target of training two million more people in digital technologies. More broadly defined services have attracted an estimated $84 billion in foreign investment over the last twenty years.[6]

With software as the economic engine, Indian businesses in other sectors also have been given room to grow. Air transport, trade, repair, restaurants and food service, machinery and equipment, and real estate all grew quickly, at double-digit rates in some years. Farmers moved into more profitable areas such as livestock and poultry as diets became more protein rich. The number of domestic passenger miles flown more than doubled in five years between 2014 and 2019. About ten to twelve million people each year moved to urban areas, boosting housing demand and construction. Even Indian manufacturing enjoyed some years of double-digit growth, especially in the food processing sectors and selected machinery and equipment. (This was not enough, however, to save the Ambassador. Hindustan Motors shut its last production line in 2014. It had been producing the same basic model for fifty-seven years.)

Rapid economic growth and urbanization sustained by a globally competitive software industry that continuously upgraded due to foreign direct investment and a world-class innovation ecosystem created a strong middle class in India. The middle class was eating better and eating out. It was taking vacations and buying houses, especially in smaller cities around the country. Almost all children in India were in school in

2020; one-quarter of those leaving high school went on to higher education. The government has set a target to double enrollment in higher education to 50 percent by 2035.

India's experience with services as the engine of economic growth has upset a century of thinking about economic development as a sequential process of moving from agriculture to manufacturing and only then to services. Before India's rise, no other country (except for a few small, tourism-dominated islands) had been able to leap instantly to a large service economy. What's more, the middle class in India did not owe its existence to direct government policy, but rather to the removal of restrictive government regulations. This creates a quite different relationship between the middle class and the political class in India compared to that in other countries.

Indian Middle-Class Values

The early development of the services sector also means that India has not followed the trajectory of modernization of beliefs laid out by political scientists Ronald Inglehart and Christian Welzel.[7] They describe a sequence in which societies transition from agrarian to industrial employment and, in so doing, start a process of shifting from traditional to more rational beliefs. In traditional societies, they argue, people take pride in their families and their country. They adapt to family and national politics rather than trying to change them. In more secular, rational societies, there is greater tolerance for differences and for individual choice to drive the pursuit of happiness, the ultimate goal of a middle-class ethos. What Inglehart and Welzel find, however, is that the transition from agriculture to the services sector does not produce the same kind of change toward secular/rational beliefs.

There is also a second dimension to the change in beliefs that occurs with modernization. That is the change from survivalism toward self-expression. Survivalist beliefs give prominence to economic and physical security above all else, and survivalist societies adopt sectarian or factional blocs to promote group security. There is little tolerance for those outside these groups. Over time, with economic development, survival becomes less important and societal beliefs shift toward tolerance, civic activism, and an emphasis on quality of life. This transition is most often associated with a shift from an industrial to a services economy. It is an explanation for why the middle class has flourished in postindustrial societies. The rational side accepts greater personal responsibility for success in life, while the self-expression dimension permits many different pathways to the good life.

In India, perhaps because it has leapfrogged over the agrarian-industrial transition phase and perhaps because of the conventions of the caste system, society remains relatively traditional. India retains strong elements of survivalism: a focus on materialism driven by science and technology and support for authoritarian government.

In the World Values Survey, Indians stand out as believing that their children should be independent and responsible, work hard, display imagination, and be thrifty, saving money and repurposing things. Determination, perseverance, and religious faith are reported to be important attributes for children to learn at home, along with unselfishness and generosity. Obedience ranks very high. Indians are reasonably satisfied with their lives but their trust in other people is low. They view making their parents proud as one of the main goals of their life. Few are active members of a civic organization, although more Indians are involved with self-help, mutual aid groups. For example, the Self-Employed Women's Association, based in India, with two million members, is one of the largest organizations of informal workers in the world.

Focus on rural, informal workers is another particularly Indian characteristic, closely linked to Gandhian philosophies of economic development. Gandhi was enamored with villages, which he believed could form the basis of self-sufficiency and decentralization. Villages could also be organized to create and partake of wealth collectively, rather than in individual family units. He favored local handicrafts over modern technologies. He believed in limiting material wants to the basic necessities, putting more store on empathy, sensitivity, and selflessness as paths to the good life.[8]

Much has changed since Gandhi's time, but his thinking still resonates in much of India, especially in its political makeup. Indian politicians spend most of their time wooing rural constituents. Most federal government financing goes to rural development, with large budget subsidies for irrigation and fertilizers, above-market government procurement prices for food grains, and guaranteed public rural employment schemes. It has been political dynamite to attempt to reform these policies. A tentative proposal in 2020 to alter government procurement of grain generated a massive protest by tens of thousands of farmers who camped outside New Delhi for several months.

With politics firmly oriented toward the poor in rural areas, the urban middle class in India is faced with a difficult choice. The economist Albert Hirschman was among the first to articulate the issue: if the group to which people belong is not useful, they face a choice between leaving the group (which he termed "exit") or trying to change things ("voice").[9] Effective voice means staying engaged. But the Indian middle class does not see engagement as useful. Politics is not important in their daily lives and the social compact between governments and the middle class, operating through a system of taxes and social benefits, is not strong in India. To illustrate, the starting threshold for a household to pay income tax is 2.5 lakh per year, roughly equal to the middle-class threshold used in this book. There are probably more than one hundred million households with incomes above this threshold, but fewer than fifteen million Indians paid any income tax in 2020, and those who did pay paid very little—a marginal tax rate of only 5 percent of their income.[10]

In other countries, taxes form a crucial part of the social compact between citizens and their governments. Citizens willingly (if somewhat grudgingly) pay taxes but expect to receive public goods and services in return. Not in India. The middle class is instead "exiting" from the state, paying almost no taxes and expecting no services. They live in their own gated communities; they have their own diesel generators for their electricity; they use private doctors and clinics and send their children to private schools. Public spending on health in India is around 1 percent of national income and total spending on health is about 3 percent. The average for a country at its stage of development would be more than 5 percent. The average for a European country is about 10 percent.[11]

According to the Indian government's *Economic Survey*, this exit has weakened both the state and the middle class.[12] The middle class is faced with having to provide basic public goods on its own, a far more expensive proposition than doing it collectively via the state. It also faces higher prices for food and housing due to state regulations and policies oriented to rural constituencies. At the same time, the state is weakened due to its focus on redistribution rather than investment. The report goes on to say: "A state that is forced into inefficient redistribution risks being trapped in a self-sustaining spiral of inefficient redistribution, reduced legitimacy, reduced resources, poor human capital investments, weak capacity and so on."[13]

The paradox of India's middle class, then, is that it is growing very rapidly, but it is not supported by, nor reinforcing, the state on which it depends. India's middle class was growing by around 15 percent per year until 2019, when the pandemic hit, and India is likely the main driving force behind the growth in the world middle-class population from three billion in 2014 to four billion in 2021. But the Indian middle class is vulnerable without the protection of the state. When the COVID-19 pandemic hit, the impact on the Indian middle class was enormous. There is optimism that the impact will be temporary and that the Indian middle class will revert to its strong growth trajectory as the pandemic recedes, but the uncertainties regarding health, economic recovery, and policy adjustments have unquestionably become much larger.

Women's Empowerment and the Indian Middle Class

No country in modern times has rapidly grown their middle class without a large percentage of women joining the workforce. There are multiple explanations for this. The simplest and most direct is that the financial contribution of women when they work outside the home is substantial, permitting two-income families to enjoy a far higher living standard than would otherwise be possible. More indirectly, and just as important from society's perspective, is the change in behavior that comes about when women work outside the home: later marriage, older mothers on average at the time of their first birth, larger spacing between births, fewer children, better educated and healthier children. Households conforming to these trends can accumulate wealth more rapidly and provide the security and resilience that is characteristic of a middle-class household.

In terms of the role of women in building the middle class, India is an exception. In 2019, only 20 percent of Indian women older than fifteen were employed. This is slightly less than its poorer Muslim neighbor, Pakistan, and slightly more than half the rate of its neighbor to the east, Bangladesh. More than two-thirds of China's women of working age are employed outside the home. The average age of a mother when she first gives birth is 20 in India and 22.7 in neighboring Pakistan (it is 29 to 30 in most of Europe). Without working women and without the support of the state, the Indian middle class is still vulnerable.

The paradox is that Indian women are well educated by the standards of many emerging market economies. More than one-quarter of women have at least a secondary education, and almost all young women are literate. Yet their likelihood of obtaining a white-collar job is low.[14] Young women are less likely to be allowed by their families to travel long distances, so job searches are narrowed. And when women marry into families with higher social status, they may be encouraged by social norms to stay at home rather than to work.

These generalizations about Indian middle-class women are supported by the findings of social science research. In a series of interviews, the American anthropologist Professor Sara Dickey finds that residents in Madurai, a city of a million people in Tamil Nadu, view the middle class as a desirable place to be, but one in which their class position is uneasy and unstable.[15] She describes how prior to the late 1990s, people were categorized into one of two groups: those who had and those who did not. There was no middle group. Only after the turn of the century did more people in Madurai start to refer to themselves as "middle people," or as belonging to a "middle family." They described "middle people" as being neat and clean, in much the same way as the Victorian journalist Isabella Beeton had extolled these as middle-class virtues a century before in a very different land.

With less of a financial contribution to the household than in other countries, the middle-class women in Madurai felt a need to behave and consume in a way denoting their middle-class status. Some scholars of the Indian middle class use such choices as a way of identifying classes—having motorized transport like a scooter is strongly correlated with being in the middle class. Lower class individuals walk or bicycle, and rich people travel by car.[16] Middle-class women felt pressure to marry their children into families with similar class status, so they paid considerable attention to conform to their local community. But this freedom of choice did not always bring satisfaction. It could cause anxiety and stress when important choices had to be made.

One pernicious aspect of choice is the sex of a child through elective abortions. Women in richer Indian states, cities, and urban areas deliver far fewer girl children than boys. These child sex ratios, as they are called in the literature, are determined by families choosing to abort female fetuses. Among the middle class, unbalanced sex ratios are more common in families with richer and more educated parents.[17] Ironically, the middle-class desire to have fewer children—modern, middle-class families have two or three children at most—creates pressures for the birth of sons. In newly emerging Indian middle-class families, the goal of a son is to enhance family income levels, whereas the goal of a daughter is to strengthen social networks and position in the community. These goals are reinforced by the practice of marriage dowries, which can be substantial and can even lead to debt among middle-class families.

Over time, as the middle class matures and becomes more established, the anxieties of newly emerging middle-class households recede. Women become empowered through their education rather than held back by social norms. But the interplay of aspirations and expectations shows how hard it can be to generate self-sustaining middle-class expansion in traditional societies.

The COVID-19 Pandemic Shrinks the Global Middle Class

The global middle class shrank during World War II. After 1946, it experienced unbroken expansion every year until 2020, when the COVID-19 pandemic hit. The pandemic and the policy response of lockdowns, social distancing, and closed borders were the largest economic shock to the global economy in seventy-five years. There was a recession in 166 countries in 2020. The size of the global economy, which had had a trend growth of 3 to 4 percent per year, actually shrank by 3.3 percent. Advanced-economy governments did everything they could to protect their middle classes. In the United States, the Coronavirus Aid, Relief and Economic Security Act (CARES Act) provided $2.3 trillion (equivalent to 85 percent of India's entire economy in 2020) in tax rebates, expanded unemployment benefits, loans, and guarantees to prevent corporate bankruptcy and to help small businesses, and other measures.[18] It has been supplemented by jobs protection programs, student loan relief, and other transfers. President Biden's American Rescue Plan has provided additional assistance to individuals and stimulus to the economy.[19]

Like the US government, most advanced-economy governments introduced large-scale fiscal and monetary stimulus programs in order to save businesses and jobs and to provide direct relief to households. The composition and size of intervention may have differed from country to country, but the objectives were largely the same. Policies were aimed at saving the middle class—saving their jobs and wages and underwriting their ability to spend. In this, the government programs have been largely successful. Even though gross domestic product fell in North America, Europe, Japan, and other advanced economies, the size of the middle class did not shrink. It may even have grown in the United States, as some upper-class households slipped back into the middle class.

The impact of COVID-19 in developing countries, however, was far more severe. Latin America was one of the most severely affected regions. Its commodity-dependent economy was hit hard by the global downturn in trade. Argentina and Ecuador defaulted on their external debt obligations. Brazil's government believed the pandemic would not significantly affect public health policy measures, and it suffered some of the worst spread of the virus.

It was India, however, where the impact on the middle class was most severe. An estimated one hundred million people fell out of the middle class in India in 2020 alone. The numbers were so high because the size of the recession in India was very large and many Indian middle-class households were near the bottom threshold. Consumer spending fell by 27 percent in the second quarter of 2020. Many of the new entrants into the middle class in India could not offset a shock of this magnitude. Their hopes and aspirations for a middle-class standard of living disappeared. The government could do little to help. Most of its assistance was targeted to rural areas: agricultural support, credit support for migrants and farmers, and higher fertilizer subsidies.

The middle class in India has recovered in 2022, although the uncertainty associated with concern about when COVID-19 might be brought under control is high. Emergence of new variants will sharply affect the speed of recovery. India is fortunate in one respect. It is already highly digitized. It has a system, the India Stack, of digital banking payments (Jan Dhan), biometric digital identification (Aadhar), and mobile connections. About 1.2 billion people, including almost all adults in India are part of this JAM (Jan Dhan bank accounts, Aadhar, and mobile) trinity. With these digital connections, Indians can receive subsidies and other services from the government in a far more effective way. Cost savings through elimination of paperwork, reduced corruption, competition among service providers, and better accountability through information-driven feedback loops are among the advantages of the stack.[20] The major benefit, however, may be indirect. The JAM stack has brought a country that initially had significant digital illiteracy into the digital age and massively broadened inclusion, especially financial inclusion of women, in the economy.

The transformation of India toward a digital economy will be a critical ingredient in the resumption of middle-class growth. The digital economy has been resilient during the pandemic everywhere in the world. In fact, the pandemic has opened a new fissure in society. The main distinctions between people and their economic interest are no longer simply oriented along the source of their income from rents, capital, or labor, but increasingly along a digital dimension. Those who were engaged in the digital economy (the "work-at-home class") were comparatively little affected by the pandemic. Those who participated in jobs requiring a physical presence in the workplace (the traditional working class) fared far worse.

In India, as in other countries, the economic interests within the middle class are fracturing along the digital divide. Until now, the core economic principles of the middle class—free trade, property rights, individual responsibility coupled with public delivery of key growth drivers like health, education, and infrastructure in an environment of reasonable taxes and low inflation—have been embraced by an ever-growing number of people. Politicians also embraced these principles, attracted by the "median voter" theory that suggests that those who are closest to the average voter, now squarely in the middle class in most countries, will do best in democratic elections. It is an agenda for growth, not for redistribution. But as extreme wealth and inequality grows, a sense of unfairness also grows. The middle class today is also voicing its concerns about discrimination, lack of inclusion, and lack of economic justice.

The tensions between these two will grow over time as the middle class becomes more financially secure and as the very wealthy grow even wealthier. The global middle class probably surpassed four billion people in 2021 or 2022. The new entrants who have made up the fourth billion of the middle class will be found to be 90 percent Asian—a combination of South Asians and East Asians. The middle class in Europe and North America will be static. In these regions, the middle class is being hollowed out, with some members transitioning to become rich, while others are losing good jobs and joining the ranks of the working class. The four billion people in the middle class will be globally integrated by trade, the internet, and social media. They will have huge computing power in their smartphones, will be more engaged in global discourse, and will be increasingly insistent on ensuring that their families and children can also look forward to a good life. Throughout the world, however, the middle class is worrying about whether it can protect its ability to live a good life.

~

Chapter 6

THE FIFTH BILLION

Pitfalls Ahead, 2022–2030

Something is rotten in the State of Denmark.

—William Shakespeare, *Hamlet*, ca. 1600

The rise of India, China, and other populous Asian countries is generating strong momentum for a continued expansion of the global middle class. Indeed, if present economic forecasts are realized, the middle class could become five billion strong by 2030. Yet the dream of sustaining the good life into the indefinite future, with so many newcomers pushing to join in, is now at risk everywhere as planetary boundaries, loss of jobs due to automation, and divisive politics of globalization and nationalism put pressure on the middle class and force a rethink of how to make it sustainable.

Denmark is often thought of as the quintessential middle-class society. Denmark ranks thirty-first in the list of billionaires per person, very low considering its wealth, and its distribution of income is among the most equal of any rich society. It has tuition-free access to high-quality education, no-fee public health care, relatively low crime and corruption levels, and a tradition of *hygge*, taking time to be with family and friends.[1] But young people in Denmark, and in Scandinavia more broadly, are afraid that the middle-class dream is slipping away from them. They are demanding action from their governments. Just as the palace guard in *Hamlet* uttered his famous quote after seeing an image of the dead king on the castle ramparts, the young Scandinavian members of the middle class are envisioning the death of their parents' way of life.

In August 2018, a fifteen-year-old Swedish schoolgirl posted pictures of herself and fellow classmates protesting the lack of action being taken by the Swedish parliament on climate change. Greta Thunberg became the face of a global movement, now numbering more than fourteen million young people, demanding changes in economic policy to protect their future.

Fridays for Future, Greta's movement, is the twenty-first-century expression of the global middle class acting in concert. For the first time, the middle class is sensing that its interests cannot be defended simply through national political action—it must globalize. The complaint is that the future of young generations is being sacrificed in order to enrich a small number of the global elite. This superclass, a group of about six thousand people who have organized economics and politics for their own interests according to political scientist and journalist David Rothkopf, has long existed but has been tolerated as long as the middle class also benefits.[2] Now, the young members of the middle class are confronting them on behalf of themselves and others even less fortunate. In the words of Greta Thunberg, "You have stolen my dreams and my childhood with your empty words. Yet I am one of the lucky ones. People are suffering."[3]

The young activists that make up Fridays for Future are voicing their concern that they will not be able to live a good life unless economic systems are radically transformed toward a path that can provide both material prosperity and a healthy planet. In the jargon of today, the children of middle-class families are doubling down on sustainable development.

Sustainable development is the new engine that must be built if the global middle class is to reach five billion people. It is a fuzzy concept that has been around for some time in policy circles. The 1987 report of the World Commission on Environment and Development, chaired by then Norwegian prime minister Gro Harlem Brundtland, described sustainable development as a process that "seeks to meet the needs and aspirations of the present without compromising the ability to meet those of the future."[4] For the middle class, this dimension of time is something they have not had to think about before. Until now, middle-class families have taken for granted the idea that their children will have more opportunities to lead the good life than they have had.

After all, wealth begets wealth, and education and health have consistently improved with each new generation. Except during periods of war or hyperinflation in some countries, the middle class steadily has seen improvements in its standard of living. But the vulnerability of the middle class has been exposed since 2010 by repeated economic, health, and social crises. Members of Generation Z—those born between the late 1990s and 2010—are the activists in Fridays for Future who worry that their chances of a good life are disappearing.

In this, Gen Z activists have a common cause with scientists. The Fridays for Future platform demands that policymakers listen to the best available science. And what science says is that the world has entered a new geological era, the Anthropocene, wherein human activity is influencing the planet to such a degree that it will be reflected forever in the fossil record embedded in rocks. For the past 11,700 years, we have been living in the Holocene era, a time marked by the retreat of the last great ice age. In 2019, scientists of the Anthropocene Working Group voted to treat the Anthropocene as a new geologic timescale defined by a global boundary stratotype section and point to be formally adopted by the International Union of Geological Sciences.[5] In plain English, these scientists believe that future generations will see a spike of new markers in rock layers caused by radioactivity, plastic pollution, and species extinction that will signal a changed planet.

The planetary changes that signal the start of the Anthropocene are a threat to economic prosperity. The global middle class's vast appetite for consumption is responsible for much of the manmade impact on the planet and so is in danger of becoming the greatest threat to itself. The global economy that serves the middle class relies on nature to a large but undocumented degree. But limits to what nature can provide are being reached and broached. Nature is changing in ways that make it more hostile to prosperity. Significant floods and tropical storms are becoming more frequent as climate change accelerates. Shortages of fresh water and insect pollinators are changing agriculture. Vast amounts of municipal solid waste are not disposed of sustainably. Mass species extinction makes for a less resilient ecology.

As if this were not bad enough, the super-rich are also inventing and embracing technologies in business models that destroy jobs. If robots and artificial intelligence remove the employment foundation of the middle class, it cannot survive. Faced with these threats, the middle class in some places is reverting to nationalism and protectionism, the politics that led it astray in the mid-twentieth century.

A fundamental question for our times is whether the middle class can continue to grow and thrive or if the children of today's middle class will find it impossible to enjoy good lifestyles. If a new sustainable growth model can be developed and put in place, there is every chance that the middle class will reach a size of at least five billion by 2030. To do this, it will have to transform economic and social processes to mitigate climate change, stay within planetary boundaries, and harness technology for broad-based social good. If the middle class wants to continue to prosper, it will have to press governments to reform a business-as-usual economy that has created prosperity in a self-destructive and unsustainable way.

Decarbonization with Middle-Class Prosperity

Young people have been talking about climate change and the environment for decades. What is new is that the framing of climate change has shifted from concern for the environment—saving the rainforests, whales, and polar bears—to concern about the well-being of one's children and grandchildren. Matthew Nisbet, former editor of the *Oxford Encyclopedia of Climate Change Communication*, lists the reasons why the climate message has become so much more compelling: "It is drama, it is novelty, it is authenticity, and it is catastrophe."[6] It is also, he might have added, intimately related to the size and potential for expansion of the middle class.

Around two-thirds of greenhouse gas (GHG) emissions in 2020 were linked to household consumption.[7] Given that the middle class accounts for three-quarters of global spending, it is responsible for about half of all GHGs. To get to a net zero world, the middle class must cut its GHG consumption per person by about 60 percent in the next decade.

It is possible to do this but only if we take four steps. Step one is to completely transform how we produce energy. The current approach is to burn fossil fuels. Despite all the attention that renewables have received in the last few years, fossil fuels still provided 81 percent of the world energy mix in 2022.[8] That is incompatible with avoiding climate change. By 2050, the share of fossil fuels in the energy mix must be reduced to no more than 15 percent. The rest must be sourced from renewables and nuclear technologies.

To see the difference this makes, consider that the level of carbon emissions by each person in France or Sweden is one-third that in the United States, largely because France produces most of its electricity using carbon-free nuclear power, whereas Sweden relies heavily on hydropower.

The decarbonization of electricity is already underway. In most parts of the world, solar energy and wind energy are cheaper than any alternative. The Saudi Arabian company ACWA won a bid to provide solar-generated electricity to the Ethiopian grid at a price of 2.5 cents per kilowatt-hour—one-third the price of electricity generated by a typical combined cycle gas turbine and one-quarter the price of a modern supercritical coal plant. The International Energy Association, a traditional advocate for the fossil fuel industry, claims that solar photovoltaics (PV) is now "the cheapest source of energy in history," at least in places where solar radiation is intense and where the cost of capital is low.[9] The only reason renewables have not yet completely replaced fossil fuels is that the intensity of the power they produce depends on the weather and the time of day. That is not good for managing an electricity load that continuously must match the supply with demand for power. In modern grids, demand is reasonably predictable according to the time of day, and supply is adjusted by the grid operator to meet it. To do this using renewables as the basic power source requires adding storage, which raises the effective cost of power considerably. Looking ahead, storage costs are coming down fast and could even be distributed to households in the form of electric car batteries or Tesla Powerwalls. Demand can also be made more flexible by time-of-day pricing, so a largely renewables-based electric grid is becoming technologically feasible and economically efficient.

Step two is to transform everything for which we use power to run on electricity: factories, cars, trains, and the heating and cooling of buildings. Ninety percent of all global energy is used for making things, going places, and controlling the temperature of the spaces where we live and work. Almost all these processes—like the low-heat requirements of food and beverage processing or textiles and garments and the medium-heat needs of drying and paint curing—can be done through electrification. In fact, one proposal is to halt all sales of fossil-fuel fired boilers by 2025 as part of the plan to accelerate electrification.

Electric cars, buses, and trucks are already on the horizon. France and other European countries also have large rail networks that people use for their daily commute as well as to get from city to city. Rail is the most efficient way of moving around. The Eurostar, the continent's famed high-speed intercity train, uses 6 grams of carbon dioxide equivalent per passenger kilometer of travel. By contrast, a short-haul domestic flight in the United States uses 255 grams. All flights are carbon intensive, but shorter ones use a disproportionate amount of energy because they have to reach cruising altitude regardless of how far they fly. For regular mobility, people will have to rely on public transport, cycling, or electric vehicles. The International Energy Agency (IEA) recommends banning the sale of vehicles with internal combustion engines after 2035.[10]

Countries with hot or cold weather need energy for heat or for air-conditioning. This is why many of the Gulf countries have among the highest carbon emissions per person. The US Department of Energy estimates that each 1 degree adjustment in the indoor temperature achieves energy savings of 1 percent over eight hours. It is also why there is a considerable risk that adding a fifth billion to the global middle class will be energy intensive. Under current scenarios of global growth, most of the new middle class would likely live in South and East Asia, areas of the world that are hot and humid and where the demand for air-conditioning is very high. Fortunately, heat pumps and energy efficient building standards can achieve considerable savings in temperature control.

The beauty of all these processes is that the low-carbon economy will end up being cheaper than current alternatives, especially if given an extra boost through government incentives. Because of this, the move to scale can happen fast and will be driven by the most powerful economic force that exists, a competitive market. Businesses that produce the old-fashioned way will face higher costs and quickly be forced to adapt or close.

Electrification does not work for everything. So, step three is to innovate new products or processes to reduce the carbon intensity of goods and services that cannot be electrified economically. For example, it is hard to think about electrifying aviation. Batteries are too heavy to carry into the sky without paying a substantial price. It is also expensive to use electricity to generate the intense heat required to make steel, cement, glass, and selected ceramics and chemicals. For these kinds of uses—representing maybe 10 to 20 percent of total energy—we either will need to continue using fossil fuels and offset emissions through carbon capture and storage or new technologies based on hydrogen or even nuclear will need to be invented.

Julio Friedman, a senior research scholar at the Center on Global Energy Policy at Columbia University, examines the challenges and policy options for the heavy industries that need intense heat to "melt rocks, mold metal, and create chemical reactions."[11] If the cheapest way of producing heat at the high temperatures needed by heavy industry (cement kilns operate at around 1,400 degrees Celsius) is to use fossil fuels, then a country that tries to switch to alternatives will simply lose the heavy industry to a competitor country that continues to use cheap fossil fuels. The solution, from an economic point of view, is an international agreement that requires all governments to tax fossil fuels to make them uneconomic to use in heavy industry. Getting an international agreement like this among all countries is difficult, so there are workarounds developed by international trade lawyers called "border tax adjustments" that would stop polluting countries from being able to freely export goods that have used, directly or indirectly, fossil fuels at any stage of the value chain.

The common element behind all of these ideas is that basic market forces could quickly reduce GHGs. In some cases, governments may need to intervene to provide the right orientation to the market and perhaps to provide the necessary infrastructure, and then businesses will respond.

Governments will only intervene to make the transformations happen if pushed by the middle class to take forceful action. The vested interests of the fossil fuel industry are huge, and they are unlikely to willingly lay down arms. They have acted before. In the United States, the Global Climate Coalition, an industry-based lobby group, promoted climate-change-skeptic research in think tanks and universities, funded by probusiness groups, for the express purpose of casting doubt on the scientific consensus about manmade climate change. Even today, 30 percent of adults in the United States believe that climate change is not real or is not caused by humans.[12] The group succeeded in blocking US ratification of the 1997 Kyoto Protocol, the first attempt at forging a global consensus on mitigating climate change, partly by creating confusion about the science, a playbook reminiscent of tobacco industry efforts to downplay the effect of smoking on cancer. Likewise, the Institute of Economic Affairs in the United Kingdom, a think tank that receives regular funding from BP, consistently downplayed the consequences of climate change. One report even claimed that climate warming would be good for the planet because of the impact on crop yields. The sums at stake are vast. The oil and gas sector accounted for more than $3 trillion of output in 2019, larger than the output of France or the United Kingdom and slightly less than the output of Germany. By delaying serious action on climate change by more than twenty years, the fossil fuel companies made plenty of money, but this all must be repaid multifold by middle-class consumers in coming years because we now have to transition even faster to a low carbon economy.

Beyond taking on vested interests, the middle class will probably need to change its own behavior. This is step four of the transition.[13] According to the International Energy Agency, more than half of the cumulative reductions in carbon emissions are linked to consumer choices. Consumers have to switch to electric vehicles, install heat pumps, change the way they commute to work, and forego flights. Who has to change the most and in which areas will vary. The patterns of middle-class consumption and middle-class energy use are quite different around the world. The average person in the US middle class, for example, emitted the equivalent of 17.6 tons of carbon dioxide in 2018, compared to 6.8 tons in France, 6.3 tons in China, and 1.7 tons in India. Much of this difference is because the middle and rich classes in the United States are wealthier than those in other countries and simply consume more, but a large part is also because of the choices that consumers in these countries make about what they eat, how they commute and travel, and how much they heat and cool their houses and offices.

Anything that depends on changing consumer behavior will be inherently unpredictable in the beginning, since there is no experience to draw on. One of the most contentious areas is about changing diets. There is no doubt that agriculture, and animal husbandry in particular, is a large contributor to carbon and methane emissions. Changing diets could help. The most extreme version of this is asking people to convert to a completely vegan diet. This would certainly save on carbon emissions, but the amount saved in one year by a person switching to a vegan diet is only about half the amount saved by taking one less long-haul plane trip. A vegetarian, Mediterranean, or similar diet would also cut carbon emissions, although not by as much as a vegan diet, partly because many vegetables can be eaten raw, eliminating the need to spend energy on cooking. There are other options too, such as moving to carbon-light meats—chicken has one-sixth the carbon footprint as lamb and one-quarter that of beef. Eating an eight-ounce steak has about the same carbon footprint as driving fifteen miles.[14]

Buying organic food saves on pesticides and fertilizers, both of which require fossil fuels to produce and transport. Shopping locally and reducing food waste also help but by decreasing amounts.

The big-ticket items might be easier to change than the smaller items. If government taxes and regulations increase the cost of air transport, for example, many people will voluntarily give up a trip or switch to rail without complaining too much. The European Commission has given France the green light to ban flights between cities connected by a train trip of less than 2.5 hours. There may be other instances when regulations can help to speed change. Consumers are creatures of habit even when better options are available to them. But when the incentives are right, change can happen fast.

As an example, think about the incandescent light bulb. In 2007, the US Congress passed a law that would prohibit, starting in 2012, the sale of light bulbs that were less than 28 percent more efficient than the existing incandescent technology, which converted only 10 percent of the energy used into light. In 2011, just before the ban was to take effect, more than two-thirds of the light bulbs in US homes were incandescent. The advent of compact fluorescents, halogens, and LED bulbs offered cheaper and better alternatives. Within five years, all but 6 percent of household bulbs had switched to one of these newer technologies. The law gave the initial impetus, but market forces augmented by utility company incentives did the trick. The fact that the old light bulbs typically died after 1.4 years also meant that all the existing stock had to be replaced: the householder's choice was not whether to replace or not, but simply with what to replace the dead bulb.

It will be harder to replace cars, boilers, and appliances with more energy efficient options than was the case for light bulbs, but the same combination of market forces, price incentives, and government regulations can work. National and local governments will be called upon to invest in the infrastructure to provide a range of alternatives so that consumers can make a reasoned choice—the rail systems and electric charging stations, for example—as well as to fund research and development on new technologies like carbon capture and underground storage. Business will be called upon to provide new energy efficient appliances, electric vehicles, and the like.

Through these measures, moving to a net zero economy is ambitious but not impossible. The gross cost of investments will be high, on the order of $5 trillion per year by 2030, according to the IEA. This is large but looks bearable when set against the almost $100 trillion of spending by the global consumer class in 2030 that is currently projected. Most important, the economics of mitigating climate change has been turned on its head. Where once it was framed as reduced consumption today in return for the promise of more (or sustained) consumption in the future, the economics have become win-win. We can have more consumption today and more consumption in the future if only there is a transition to a low-carbon path.

The net economic benefits of this transition are what will support the continued expansion of the middle class. The middle class will benefit through lower prices for most goods and services, thanks to the falling cost of electricity based on renewables. They may pay higher taxes on goods that are still produced with fossil fuels, but much of those taxes will be borne by rich households and shareholders of capital-intensive businesses. Meanwhile, better health due to lower air pollution and a slowdown of climate change benefit everyone, and since the middle class is already the majority of the world's population, they gain the most from mitigating climate change.

Protecting Nature and Reducing Middle-Class Waste

In addition to decarbonizing economic systems, another needed transformation is to stop harming the natural environment. Across the world, we simply must produce and throw away less stuff. Our economic system uses a "take-make-dispose" process that required ninety-two billion metric tons of raw materials in 2017, or 12.2 tons per person on average.[15] Given that poor people spend less than average, the average person in the middle class probably uses twenty tons per year of material to satisfy their consumption. That is about one's own bodyweight, every single day. More than two billion tons per year has to be disposed of by municipalities. Despite all the composting and recycling efforts in place, at least one third of this trash is not managed sustainably. In developing countries, where middle class growth is most rapid, half of all waste is openly dumped.[16]

Waste is unsightly and a health hazard, and the organic matter contained within it decomposes and contributes to climate change. It also damages the planet's ecosystems. The Great Pacific Garbage Patch, floating between San Francisco and Hawaii, is a million square miles (twice the size of France) and contains eighty thousand tons of garbage, about half of which is discarded fishing gear. A rule of thumb, proposed by the oceanographer Charles Moore who discovered the phenomenon, is that the patch will double its size every decade.

If the middle class is to continue to grow, the problem of waste disposal must be solved. It is a new problem because of the global spread of the middle class. When the middle class was concentrated in rich countries, waste was simply exported to developing countries: China, India, and Malaysia among others were paid to take the trash of the

Global North. But as the middle class has grown in these countries, they have toughened regulations on the import of waste, while at the same time they have had to deal with their own domestically produced waste. The old system has broken down. A new system, called the "circular economy," is still being invented.

The circular economy is a concept that designs out waste and pollution, recycles materials, and regenerates the natural environment.[17] The recycling part is familiar to most people, but what is new in the circular economy concept are the design and regeneration phases.

For many years now, recycling has been an important element in selected areas. Aluminum, for example, can be recycled indefinitely without losing its properties, so an estimated three-quarters of all aluminum ever produced is still in use. By comparison, only 9 percent of plastic remains in use. This does not necessarily mean that aluminum is better or greener. It takes a lot of energy to produce it in the first place, although far less to process it after it has been recycled. In fact, the reason why so much aluminum is recycled is precisely because it is so much cheaper to make a new can of recycled aluminum compared to new aluminum.

Many other metals fall into the same category as aluminum. Gold is used in many electronic components, and it stands to reason that a lot of effort would be put into making sure that when these parts are disposed of, all the gold is recycled. As a general proposition, the new digital economy uses a lot of metals—copper wiring, lithium batteries with cobalt cathodes, and many others. Metals are the wave of the future. The most precious resources for the global economy are shifting. The global economic cheering squad is replacing "drill, baby, drill" with "dig, baby, dig."

The inherent value of metals makes recycling them a sound business venture. The same is true for other products. Almost 60 percent of paper is produced with recycled material. But this is not the case for plastics. It is quite cheap to produce plastic compared with the cost of recycling; half of the three hundred million tons of plastics produced each year is used only once for things like grocery bags, straws, bottles, takeout cutlery, and packaging. All of this is then thrown away, mostly into landfills, but much of it—fourteen million metric tons in 2020—

finds its way into the oceans. The World Economic Forum estimates that there will be more plastic in the oceans in 2050 than fish.

The first plastic recycling plant was built in Conshohocken, Pennsylvania, in 1972. The ubiquitous triangle, indicating which plastics can and cannot be recycled, was introduced in 1988. Despite fifty years of history, only about 10 percent of plastics are recycled. The rest gradually break up into ever smaller pieces that are then ingested by wildlife and fish (and ultimately humans). The plastics are not benign, and there is considerable evidence to suggest that some of the chemicals they contain, such as per- and polyfluoroalkyl substances (PFAs), accumulate over time in the body and are a health hazard.

As long as plastics are produced in their current form, there is no realistic chance of them being recycled more completely. The economics are not persuasive and the consumer behavior and change that is required is hard to achieve on the necessary scale. So what can be done about the plastics problem? The answer lies in design.

One new branch of design finds substitutes for plastics. Paper straws are a good example; using old-style cloth shopping bags are another. Consumers can be persuaded to use these substitutes through a combination of government regulations and incentives. The first country to ban plastic bags was Bangladesh. That country experiences periodic flooding due to its low-lying geography and exposure to cyclones. The impact of floods on cities can be mitigated by channeling the water away, but when plastics block these channels, the systems are ineffective. After a particularly bad flood in 2002, Bangladesh banned the use of plastic and polyethylene bags, which were clogging its waterways. Since then, according to the United Nations, sixty-nine countries have put in place full or partial bans on plastic bags, including several large countries such as China, France, and Italy. The enforcement of the ban, however, has been patchy, including in Bangladesh. Most European countries and Japan, therefore, charge a fee or tax on the use of plastic bags as a monetary incentive for consumers to reduce their use. But in some places, notably the United States, there is no consensus about what to do. California and Hawaii have instituted a ban; the District of Columbia charges a fee; New York and other eastern states have advanced recycling and reuse programs;

and Florida, Arizona, and a number of Midwestern states simply have denied the existence of a problem and have preemptively banned any form of government regulation on plastic bags.

One focus of new design, especially for plastic packaging, which is one of the largest uses of plastics, is to substitute single-use plastic with materials that can be reused. To make this economically viable, there must be an after-use market for the new materials. That, in turn, can best happen when there is an infrastructure in place to identify, separate, and sort materials so they can be reprocessed in an efficient way. A European strategy for plastics looks to make all plastic packaging recyclable by 2030.[18]

Much of the innovation for the circular economy comes from new business models and practices. Imagine if a company does not buy the carpeting for its office but simply rents it. The supplier provides tiles with adhesive backing, and when it is time to replace the old carpeting (or a single soiled tile), the company removes and recycles it itself. Because the carpet supplier has full control over the materials it uses, it has an incentive to develop products that can be readily reprocessed. This is now the norm in many advanced economies. The Dutch company Interface Europe publicly committed to using 100 percent renewable energy and 100 percent recycled and biobased materials for its flooring designs and materials. It already has reduced material waste by using a new ultrasonic cutting machine and has reduced its water and gas consumption using new technologies. None of its products made and sold in its European operations end up in a landfill.

The ultimate test of the circular economy will be to regenerate nature, not simply to avoid destroying it. This is technically feasible. For example, Newlight, a California-based company that started in 2018, has developed a technology to convert methane and carbon dioxide from the air into a biomaterial called polyhydroxybutyrate, or PHB, which can be used as a substitute for plastic, fiber, and leather. It calls its material AirCarbon. Another company, San Francisco–based MycoWorks, is producing a material that can substitute for either plastics or fabrics. Mycelium is an underground network of fungal bodies from which mushrooms grow. One such network in Oregon is already the largest known living organism in the world. It can be grown naturally and pressed and dyed to mimic any kind of animal leather, from cowhide to crocodile. Bags, shoes, belts, and other fashion accessories can be made of it. At the end of its life, the material is biodegradable and compostable. Compared to animal leather, mycelium saves on water and energy and does not require the hazardous chemicals used in tanning.

The oceanic microorganisms that are used in AirCarbon and the fungi used in mushroom leather are examples of how nature can contribute to human welfare. It is not hard to find other examples of ecological services provided by nature. They range from rainforest and underwater kelp carbon sinks to coastal protection from mangroves and coral reefs. Coffee, cocoa, almonds, and many other fruits and vegetables rely on insect pollination. Seventy percent of drugs used to treat cancer are natural or synthetic compounds inspired by nature. All these examples are offered to us for free by nature. Perhaps that is why they are so underappreciated and now are under threat. Land, oceans, and wetlands everywhere on the planet have been severely altered by humans. One consequence is the possible extinction of up to one million species within decades, or one-quarter of all assessed animal and plant groups.[19] If that happens, the chances for a continued expansion of the middle class will fall dramatically. Certainly, the middle-class values of living a good life in harmony with nature—the idea of Mother Earth, which almost all cultures of the world embrace—would be destroyed.

We are, in fact, living at a time of the sixth mass extinction of life, one that scientists worry is the most serious threat to civilization because it could be irreversible.[20] Mass extinctions have happened before, although not often—about once every eighty million years. They have been caused by massive volcanic eruptions and by asteroid collisions. This one, however, is being caused by humans, largely to cater to the wants of the global middle class. The mass of all humans and their domesticated animals is now thirty times larger than the mass of all living wild animals, which simply are being pushed out of their natural habitat and can no longer find the natural resources to sustain themselves.

Scientists believe that the rate of species extinction today is more than one hundred times faster than what would have been predicted based on the historical record.[21] For the most part, the news of species extinction passes unnoticed or with a shake of the head and a moment of sorrow for the average citizen. When Lonesome George, the last giant tortoise of the Pinta Island species, died in 2012, there was a flurry of news reports, but few people saw a direct connection to their own lives. Although hard data on species populations is not complete, it seems that there are more than nine hundred vertebrate species with fewer than five thousand individuals still alive. The concern is that as those species become extinct, they will change the ecosystem where they live, threatening other species and generating an accelerating spiral of extinctions.

Paradoxically, the success of the middle class and its growing consumption has contributed to this threat of species extinction. Land-use change for agriculture, animal husbandry, and creation of cities has had the largest impact on nature, followed by overexploitation of resources by fishing, hunting, harvesting, and logging at unsustainable rates.

This is why there is increasing focus on changing the trends for how land is used. The answer to the question, "Can we provide healthy, safe, and affordable food for everyone without converting more land to agricultural use?" is, quite simply, "Yes, but only if we make several changes." Foremost among these is how we get our proteins. The basic facts are simple: less than half the world's cereals are fed to humans. The rest goes to feeding animals and for biofuels. In the United States and Australia, the share is even lower: around 10 percent of cereals are eaten by humans. It is the demand for meat and dairy that pushes farmers to cut down forests in order to plant more crops. Half the world's habitable land has been converted for agricultural use, and most of this is for raising livestock, either directly by allowing cattle to graze or indirectly by growing corn and soybeans to feed to cattle.[22] If you combined all the land used for meat and dairy, it would cover the Americas from Alaska to Tierra del Fuego.

Much of this land could be restored to nature, thereby protecting innumerable species. If everyone shifted to a vegan diet, we would need a bit more cropland to grow our food, but we would be able to give back to nature three billion of the four billion hectares of crop and pastureland that humans currently control.

Forcing everyone to shift to a vegan diet might be extreme. Imagine that instead we include eggs, chicken, pork, and fish in our diets. This would require only 10 percent more land than a vegan diet. Even if dairy—milk and cheese—is left on the menu, we could still take two billion hectares out of agriculture. That is an area almost as large as all of North America.

What would be done with those two billion hectares? About half a billion hectares would be suitable for closed forest restoration, which would help to slow climate change and to save species. The other 1.5 billion hectares would have a mosaic of uses: protected reserves, ecological corridors, agroforestry systems, and riparian plantings to protect waterways.[23] Even some small-scale farming and human settlements could be included. This kind of conservation restoration is already being implemented in some places. The key is to do so at scale.

The science behind these ideas has been aggregated into a Global Deal for Nature, initially a proposal by scientists to ask every country in the world to formally protect 30 percent of its landmass by 2030, with an additional 20 percent designated as climate stabilization areas.[24] This is no longer a wild idea; all nations of the world adopted a global biodiversity framework incorporating these and other goals in December 2022 under the auspices of the United Nations. Implementation has already started in the United States through an executive order issued by President Biden in January 2021. Although the order does not have the force of law, it instructs the Department of the Interior to draw up plans to achieve the goal; the blueprint is called "America the Beautiful." It will need to be ambitious. The United States protected only 12 percent of its land in 2022, well short of the target.

These levers to reduce biodiversity loss are grounded in the idea that a good quality of life does not necessarily entail ever-increasing consumption of the things we now eat. It simply means shifting to sensible and sustainable patterns of consumption. Indigenous and local communities have deep knowledge of how to put this into practice, and partnerships between governments and these communities are being created as a key implementation mechanism. The trade-off for the middle class is simple. Give up eating beef, lamb, and mutton, and stop mass extinctions. Luckily for the planet, many of the new members of the middle class are in India, where most protein already comes from plants and where eating beef is culturally taboo for Hindus. And for those people who simply cannot imagine a good life without a steak, there are new forms of lab-cultured meat that will be indistinguishable in taste to what is now available from animals—though it will probably be more expensive.

Decent Work and Job Security for the Middle Class

Governments everywhere are obsessed with creating jobs—not just any old job but good jobs or, as it is sometimes called, decent work. Decent work offers a fair income, workplace security, protections for families against economic shocks, and prospects for personal development. It is the basis for a middle-class lifestyle. The problem is that businesses are determined to keep wages as low as possible. Whenever they can, businesses replace people with robots or computers that perform the same tasks more reliably and more cheaply. Thankfully, economic history suggests that losing jobs in some sectors is not a problem but a sign of success. Alarm clocks are a clear advance compared with employing people to wake you up—that is why the profession of the knocker-upper, someone who tapped on windows or used pea shooters to deliver a rat-a-tat call to get industrial workers to their morning shift on time, lasted for about only one century; the last knocker-upper in London retired in the 1970s.[25]

So why the angst now about jobs? Why don't young people intuitively feel that they too will benefit from the new and hopefully more exciting and creative jobs that a technologically advanced society has to offer? The answer may lie in the deep-rooted culture of work in Christian tradition. Back in 1891, Pope Leo XIII discussed the nature of work and technology in his *Rerum novarum*, laying out a doctrine that work should provide a decent life for workers and their families. Ninety years later, Pope John Paul II reflected further on the relationship between man and work in *Laborem exercens*. His interpretation of the Genesis command to "fill the earth and subdue it" is that work is an essential part of the fulfillment of the human being.[26] John Paul, however, is careful to distinguish between work and toil, the hard labor to which man is condemned because Adam listened to the words of Eve and ate the forbidden fruit in defiance of God's commandment. Work is part of an uplifting process of self-realization. Toil is the atonement for sin. Lutherans have expressed similar views; "work constitutes a fundamental aspect of human existence . . . human beings find deep satisfaction when their work and creativity are recognized by others."[27] Work is now enshrined in the Universal Declaration of Human Rights (article 23): "Everyone has the right to work, to free choice of employment, to just and favourable conditions of work and to protection against unemployment."[28]

From this perspective, technology is an ally of man when it "facilitates, perfects, accelerates and augments his work."[29] It is his enemy when it reduces him to the "status of its slave."[30] Most of the technological advances of the last two centuries have fallen into the former category, with machines by and large replacing repetitive, routine, or manual labor. Yet there is a sense today that this is changing; technology could be replacing more creative aspects of work. Already machines have conquered humans at chess and Go, two of the most strategic games ever invented. Now many are wondering if machines will be awarded the Nobel Prize for medicine in the near future.[31] Business leaders speculate whether artificial intelligence can and should be given a seat in boardrooms. The Hong Kong–based Deep Knowledge Ventures gave an algorithm called "VITAL" observer status on its board of directors and, although widely dismissed as a publicity stunt, the core idea that an algorithm could help decipher patterns in the characteristics of a successful biotechnology company no longer sounds like pure science fiction.

Recent trends in labor markets in advanced economies reinforce this concern that only a few humans will be able to enjoy work while most others will be condemned to toil. In 2011, a report by the International Monetary Fund looked at the labor markets in all advanced economies.[32] It broke down jobs into high-wage, middle-wage, and low-wage levels and then asked which category of jobs grew fastest between 1993 and 2006. The answer: the high-wage and low-wage segments. Every one of the eighteen countries in the study showed a decline in job growth at middle-wage levels.

In some countries, the jobs outcome was unambiguously bad: Finland, Ireland, and Portugal all showed a rise in low-wage jobs that almost exactly corresponded to the fall in middle-paying jobs. The middle class suffered there. In other countries, however, the outcome was good. In Austria, Italy, France, Luxembourg, and Germany, the decline in middle-paying jobs was accompanied by a decline in low-paying jobs and a corresponding rise in high-paying jobs. The middle class gained access to better jobs. In the other countries, the pattern was mixed. The fall in middle-paying jobs was offset by a rise in both high-paying and low-paying jobs. This kind of evidence has been described as the "hollowing out" of the middle class. It reflects the fall in numbers of clerks and assistants, machine operators, middle management, and intermediaries of all kinds, from travel agents to small shopkeepers and independent bookstore owners. When thinking about the hollowing-out phenomenon, however, it is important to recognize that as many people are transitioning from the middle class to become rich as are falling out of the middle class into a lower class.

Economists fiercely debated why this happened, whether it is because of technology and globalization, which led to the offshoring of many manufacturing jobs to developing countries, or whether it is because of a gap in skills needed for the workforce of the future. After all, technology still seems to be a ticket to prosperity at the national level. The McKinsey Global Institute believes that accelerating adoption of new technology will raise productivity in advanced economies by 1 percent per year (more than doubling the pre-pandemic rate).[33] It argues that the shift to e-commerce, automation, and the closure of less efficient plants will have long-lasting positive effects, particularly in sectors like health care, which have long suffered from low productivity growth. This positive news has helped boost the value of middle-class assets in housing and stock markets.

However, the mechanisms that for decades have ensured that the benefits of productivity growth would be broadly shared in society are no longer delivering income growth for the middle class. In the United States, productivity has grown four times faster than hourly compensation in the forty-year time span between 1979 and 2019. The implication of this trend is that even if the middle class were to re-skill through retraining or higher education, it is unclear how much of the benefits of higher productivity would be reflected in their paychecks.

Two ladders of the middle class in some advanced economies are being pushed aside, especially in the United States and the United Kingdom: the ladder for advancement for individuals during their own lifetime and the ladder for the advancement of their children.

From the point of view of an individual middle-class wage or salary earner, a decent job is one that offers fair pay as well as prospects for personal advancement. It is rare for anyone to have the same job for their whole career or even to work for the same company. A distinguishing feature of a good job is what it does for one's future prospects. The middle-class experience has always been associated with upward mobility. Individuals were able to get ahead by working their way up in their own sector (or cluster of occupations).

Within the United States, new data permits the mobility of individuals to be traced. A Brookings Institution study of 228,000 real occupation-to-occupation transitions in 130 sectors shows how upward and downward mobility is affected by one's starting point.[34] Two contrasting examples illustrate the point. Imagine two equal-sized groups of workers, each earning $12 per hour, half working in retail sales and the other half as personal care aides. The study authors looked at the next job of these people. Two-thirds of the retail salespeople moved to a better job as a supervisor, a customer service representative, or even an executive. The other one-third were forced into less well-paying jobs, as cashiers or waitstaff, for example. By contrast, only one-third of the personal care aides got better jobs, like becoming nurses, social workers, or counselors, while two-thirds moved to similar or worse paying jobs—child-care workers, house or building cleaners. From the perspective of mobility, the retail sales jobs are "better" than the jobs as a personal care aide.

By looking at these transitions over hundreds of occupations, the authors were able to identify which jobs offer the best prospects for upward mobility and which are low mobility or stagnant occupations. Those with upward mobility correspond most closely to the definition of good work, in which fulfillment occurs in the form of self-improvement over time. Jobs with stagnant or low mobility are closer to the concept of toil. They provide an income stream, but little in the way of hope for improvement.

By classifying jobs and occupations in this way, the meaning of the hollowing out of the middle class becomes more tangible. It is not simply a matter of what is happening to the level of wages, it is also about the ladder to success.

The second ladder of mobility, the intergenerational ladder, has also lengthened. In the United States, for example, where the narrative of the American dream being achievable through hard work and self-responsibility is still strongly believed, social mobility has been steadily falling since World War II. Raj Chetty, a Harvard University professor of economics, found that by 2014 the share of thirty-year-olds making more than their parents did at the same age had fallen to 50 percent; in 1975, that share had been 85 percent.[35] As a result, only 9 percent of American men in the top quartile of earners had a father from the bottom quartile.[36] This has not always been true, nor is it the rule in every country. But in more and more European countries, including Austria, France, Germany, Ireland, and Luxembourg, if you are a man whose father was in the bottom quartile of income earners, the chance of moving into the top quartile of income earners is roughly half the chance of staying in the bottom.

This is a disturbing statistic for middle-class families who believe that individual effort—hard work and natural ability—is the prime factor behind success. It undercuts the belief that there is a ladder to success for everyone. That belief is behind the enormous pride in most middle-class families when their children graduate from college or gain professional qualifications. Like in a snakes and ladders game, a higher education has long been considered a clear ladder to prosperity. Now it is less clear. Luck or built-in barriers to mobility seem just as important.

What determines who will be lucky as technology evolves and who will not be so lucky? One approach is to categorize jobs along two dimensions. There are jobs that rely on "brains" and those that rely on "brawn," or, more technically, cognitive and manual jobs. In each case, the jobs can be further subdivided into those in which routine and nonroutine tasks are carried out. Financial managers and software engineers are examples of cognitive nonroutine jobs. Administrative assistants, clerks, and data entry coders would be placed in the cognitive routine category. On the manual side, construction workers, care assistants, and janitors would be classified as having nonroutine occupations, whereas forklift drivers and welding and metal pressing operators perform routine tasks.

The routine versus nonroutine breakdown corresponds better with tasks than with jobs. Every job has some routine components and some nonroutine components. From the perspective of the middle class, as long as technology replaced the routine components of jobs and permitted more time to be spent on the nonroutine components, it was a good thing to be encouraged. Jobs would not be lost; they would be upgraded. Data from labor force surveys suggest this is exactly what has been happening to middle-class jobs since the 1980s. The jobs that have been declining are those in middle-wage, routine occupations, both cognitive and manual. The declines are not steady over time, but heavily concentrated during periods of economic recession. This makes the adjustments sharper and more visible—many affected workers are looking to transition at the same time—and thus more challenging for policymakers.

Occupational mobility has provided the solution to the challenge of technology replacing routine tasks. People have changed jobs and occupations during periods of recovery from economic recession. Not everyone has been able to do this, especially when geographic or other barriers to mobility intervene, but for the vast majority of the middle class, especially those living in urban areas offering a wide array of jobs, mobility has been the response to technological change.

Economists have favored linking mobility with retraining and skills development. They refer to the new technologies as "skill-biased technical change."[37] Advances in personal computing and information technology have improved the productivity of and demand for knowledge workers. Even though the supply of college educated graduates has also increased, it has not been fast enough (or in the right science, technology, engineering, and math disciplines), so the wage premium for skilled workers has risen. If workers can be "upskilled," then the new technologies can accelerate prosperity.

Unfortunately, it is not so easy to upskill. During the COVID-19 pandemic, as with previous recessions, large numbers of people were laid off, especially in those service-oriented sectors that required face-to-face interactions. Travel and hospitality, hotels and restaurants, and airlines were severely affected. Many jobs in these sectors will not come back and those who were employed in them will be forced onto new pathways. In some cases, the new jobs will offer worse prospects than before.

Other people, by and large knowledge workers and salaried professionals in the upper middle class, have had a radically different lived experience during the pandemic. The financial services and tech sectors were unaffected by the lockdowns. Many workers were able to continue without noticeable impact on their work simply by accessing the internet and connecting online with peers, suppliers, and customers. As economies emerge from the COVID-19-created recession, it seems that technology is a boon for this group, most of whom are in the middle class.

Until the 2020s, the prevailing attitude toward technology has reflected this idea of technology as beneficial for the middle class. But a new form of technological change is emerging—artificial intelligence (AI). What is different about AI compared to previous technologies is that it is competing with good, nonroutine work rather than with toil. Hans Moravec, author, entrepreneur, and faculty member at the robotics institute of Carnegie Mellon University, put it crisply as a paradox: "It is comparatively easy to make computers exhibit adult level performance . . . and difficult or impossible to give them the skills of a one-year-old."[38] The simple skills that every toddler learns instinctively—movement, speech, perception—are far harder to teach a computer than the more complex skills of logical reasoning. For example, AI cannot yet read handwriting but is able to suggest new ways of predicting disruptive instabilities in controlled nuclear fusion plasmas.[39] Simply put, AI is disrupting decent work (cognitive nonroutine tasks) rather than toil.

This is the new challenge for the middle class. AI's ability to perform cognitive tasks is unprecedented. The best-case scenario is that it could release an outpouring of creativity that will enhance personal satisfaction. But it could also lead to the substitution of skilled workers and an acceleration in the hollowing out of the middle class.

Absent social approval, there could be a broad-based call for governments to slow down or better regulate the introduction of new technologies. Societal ambivalence toward technology is a long-standing phenomenon. More than two hundred years ago, the Luddites rampaged through Nottinghamshire, England, breaking textile machines. In response, Parliament passed the Frame Breaking Act of 1812, making such acts capital offenses. Faced with death if caught, the Luddites, unsurprisingly, became a secret society, taking their name from a possibly mythical leader they referred to as General Ned Ludd.

The spirit of Luddism is alive and well in the middle class today, with ever-larger calls to regulate big tech. A coalition is building among industry sectors opposed to globalization and a green economy, blue collar workers opposed to automation, and others worried about personal privacy and the ethics of AI. The nationalist, protectionist, and expanded role of government that this coalition represents would damage the long-term prospects for the middle class.

The middle class instead needs to coalesce around the idea that it should aspire to cognitive tasks, with AI as a complement rather than a substitute for knowledge workers. It needs to make sure that these jobs are well remunerated, something that is not currently true in all cases. Care aides, for example, do not yet receive the remuneration levels that they need to be full members of the middle class. The idea that they get a market wage, and therefore as much as they deserve, does not seem to hold up to the evidence showing productivity levels diverging from wages, probably because of power imbalances between individual workers and large corporations. These can be influenced by minimum wage legislation, unions, and other labor market institutional reforms, a new agenda for the middle class.

If the middle class cannot find common ground with each other along these lines, it risks bifurcating into two: a group of well-educated, largely upper-middle-class salaried professionals in the digital economy and a working class in the care economy. Although both will be performing cognitive tasks, they will have quite different economic interests. If that happens, the middle class—as a reasonably united political group pushing to keep taxes low and prices down (often through free trade) and taking responsibility for its own success through hard work—will splinter. Its successes in getting governments to spend tax money on education, health, old age pensions, and personal security and justice could be compromised. The rich and upper middle class will instead try to shift the agenda to lower corporate income taxes and limited capital gains taxes through estate and inheritance loopholes and the like.

The question asked at the start of this chapter is "Will the middle class continue to expand and reach five billion in the near future?" The answer is yes, but only if it resolves some of the tensions that threaten the unity of the middle class's economic agenda. It has to build a coalition that will tackle climate change and preserve nature, and this requires intergenerational solidarity, not just solidarity among workers (and voters) today. It has to embrace technology and the creative work of the future, while taking care of those adversely affected by the transition. It has to generate new bridges between high-skill and low-skill cognitive workers to keep their political power intact, and this will require reducing the wage inequalities between these types of jobs.

Above all, the middle class needs to reimagine what the good life means. Today, middle-class consumers buy a lot and travel a lot. Their carbon footprint is high in almost everything they do. The middle-class diet is rich in protein, much of which is sourced from beef and lamb. But cows and sheep release a lot of methane. The middle class live in spacious dwellings that they like to maintain at a constant, comfortable temperature. The heating and cooling uses a lot of power, still largely derived from fossil sources. The middle class likes to travel. Owning a car and vacationing each year is part of the lifestyle. Each is carbon intensive; flying is the most carbon intensive form of transport available and the fastest growing segment of travel. These middle-class habits have been tolerated for the last two centuries by simply emitting carbon into the atmosphere. For a while, it did not matter. The concentrations of carbon were too small to make a difference.

Building a green, nature-preserving, good-jobs-creating economy is now the existential challenge for the middle class. If it succeeds, and there is every technical reason to suppose it can, the middle class will continue to thrive and expand globally. But the challenges to maintaining a big-tent middle-class are greater than they have been since the early days of the nineteenth century when the middle class was just starting to achieve political power.

Chapter 7

A NEW AGENDA FOR THE GLOBAL MIDDLE CLASS

Well-Being for Five Billion People

> It will be those peoples, who can keep alive, and cultivate into a fuller perfection, the art of life itself and do not sell themselves for the means of life, who will be able to enjoy the abundance when it comes.
>
> —John Maynard Keynes, 1930[1]

In 1930, John Maynard Keynes speculated that the economic problem—scarcity of material goods and a struggle for subsistence—would be solved in one hundred years. But he warned that that would not necessarily bring happiness. He wrote, "I think with dread of the readjustment of the habits and instincts of the ordinary man, bred into him for countless generations, which he may be asked to discard within a few decades."[2] He could have been talking about the middle class of today. In many countries, the middle class has largely achieved freedom from want, but in doing so, it has been conditioned to work longer and longer hours to generate more income. It has also seen the effects of its consumerism on climate change and on the destruction of nature. The middle-class lifestyle of today is no longer satisfying, and the happiness that the middle class seeks is still elusive.

The idea that money cannot buy happiness was introduced into the academic discourse by the American economist Richard Easterlin in the mid-1970s. The Easterlin paradox, as it is called, states that happiness does not increase with a country's income level in the long run, although at any given time, within and across countries, happiness is linked to incomes. Originally based on data for the United States, Easterlin's findings have been corroborated for Europe and Japan and, in 2010, for a number of developing countries by Easterlin and colleagues.[3]

Easterlin's paradox is based on long-run findings. He concurs with the general literature that short-term deviations in the economic cycle—booms and busts—are linked to similar changes in happiness. His point is simply that "raising the incomes of all does not lead to raising the happiness of all."[4] The finding is controversial, to say the least. Other notable economists have claimed to debunk it. Nobel laureates Daniel Kahneman and Angus Deaton offer a more nuanced version: "We conclude that higher incomes buy life satisfaction but not happiness," their point being that happiness is a multifaceted concept and statistical relationships with one element of happiness may not hold true for other elements. The Deaton-Kahneman work also suggests that the ability of income to contribute to higher emotional well-being only operates below $75,000. After that, additional income does not lead to better well-being.[5] Even if the marginal well-being from income does not fall to zero, as Deaton and Kahneman suggest, there is broad agreement in the profession that it declines as incomes rise, implying that the well-being benefits from a given income gain are larger when income levels are low.

From the perspective of the middle class, the major idea that these academic studies raise is that money is only one dimension of the good life. It is the dimension that policymakers have emphasized since the start of the Industrial Revolution, but it may not be the main driver of middle-class satisfaction in the modern world. This idea is corroborated by the longest study of well-being, the Harvard Study of Adult Development. Originally designed to trace the health and life experiences of Harvard sophomores in 1938, at the height of the Great Depression, the study has since been expanded to include their offspring and outside control groups. There is a rich body of data and experiences yielding many insights, but the most striking finding is that the strength of people's relationships is the key to the good life. The study found that satisfaction with one's relationships at age fifty was a better predictor of health at age eighty than, for example, levels of cholesterol. It also found that relationships were a better predictor of contentment than money, fame, social class, IQ, or genes.[6] Thankfully, the study has also debunked the racist ideas that body measurements and genetics determined life outcomes, which were being pursued at the time by Harvard professors like William Sheldon.

With the contentment and stability of the middle class under threat, policymakers are scrambling to discover how to build a middle class that can live the good life in all its senses. Whoever succeeds in this will win the great geopolitical competition between the United States, Europe, China, and other countries that is unfolding. The victor in this fight will not be the country with the largest and strongest military force or even the strongest economy. It will be the country where the majority of its citizens—the middle class—believes its government has chosen a set of policies that address their aspirations, the country that the middle class of other nations is envious of and wants to emulate. It is the middle-class search for happiness that promises to bring about the change that is needed to put global economic systems onto a path of sustainable and inclusive growth.

In this battle, the old labels of capitalism and communism, conservative and liberal are no longer relevant. Those terms largely relate to the fight over economics and material well-being, which, though important, are no longer the key determinant of social progress. Instead, a more nuanced language of well-being is emerging that more closely resembles the ancient Greek idea of the good life. This language is common to the middle class in advanced economies as well as to the newly emerging middle class in Asian and other developing countries.

The middle class of the twenty-first century is searching for a new narrative. The last two centuries have been unbelievably successful in delivering material prosperity—more consumption of goods and services—and in delivering a life of stability, security, and respect. This progress has rested on the narrative of an individual's personal ability to take responsibility and plan for their own future. The freedom to plan and make individual choices, in turn, is at the core of the middle-class narrative of the last two hundred years: how to live when freed from the constant struggle for survival. The middle class has built itself through hard work and determination but looked to the government to provide services that are more efficiently done as a collective: public health and education, safety nets against shocks of sickness, unemployment, or disability. It is possible for individual families to take care of their own health, education, and even insurance (by saving), and some have taken this path, but it is far more efficient to do this on a collective scale through local or national governments.

Money helps a middle-class family, of course, but it is not sufficient to deliver a good life. It turns out that there are other roles for the government in helping create an environment where the middle class can thrive. A middle-class life should have minimal stress, it should provide a high degree of satisfaction with life and hope for the future, and it should impart a sense of purpose and meaning to one's activities. A middle-class lifestyle that embodies these principles is one that is also compatible with a low-carbon, nature friendly, and inclusive society.

These issues are only now coming to the forefront of policymakers' attention, partly because, in the past, national statistical systems collected data only on economic growth rather than on subjective well-being, so policymakers did not understand the source and depth of middle-class unhappiness.

This is now starting to change. In 2010, the UK Office for National Statistics introduced a program to measure national well-being along ten domains, including subjective measures of personal satisfaction with life, relationships, and sense of purpose at work and in one's spare time. New Zealand introduced a well-being budget in 2019, becoming the first country to explicitly prioritize mental health in its government spending plan. The Organization for Economic Cooperation and Development has a Better Life Index that permits comparisons of its member countries along a range of indicators going beyond consumption, such as sense of community, civic engagement, life satisfaction, and work-life balance. A World Happiness Report has been produced annually since 2013 by an independent group of experts commissioned by the United Nations in response to the Bhutanese Resolution inviting national governments to "give more importance to happiness and well-being in determining how to achieve and measure social and economic development."[7] In its 2021 report, it lists Finland, Denmark, Switzerland, and Iceland as the happiest countries in the world, while Zimbabwe and Afghanistan are the least happy. The United States ranks 19th, China 84th, and India 139th. In each of the last three examples, the happiness index is below the corresponding index of economic health, or per capita gross domestic product (GDP). The analysis in the report suggests that income levels, social support, healthy life expectancy at birth, freedom to make life choices, generosity, and the absence of corruption are all factors explaining the differences in happiness across countries.

The new metrics are promoting changes in how societies are organized and in how government money is being spent. The new agenda for the middle class is to ensure that its issues are prioritized by the government.

The academic constructs of well-being revolve around distinct sets of subjective data.[8] One data set is about the moods and emotions of daily living: hedonic indicators measuring people's responses to questions about whether they smile or frown or feel stressed or anxious. A second type of data is about people's sense of satisfaction with life as a whole: ladder-of-life type questions that ask people to evaluate how well they think things are going in their lives. The most famous of these is the Cantril Self-Anchoring Striving Scale, developed in 1965 by Princeton psychologist Dr. Hadley Cantril, who posed the following question to subjects: "Please imagine a ladder with steps numbered from zero at the bottom to ten at the top. The top of the ladder represents the best possible life for you and the bottom of the ladder represents the worst possible life for you. On which step of the ladder would you say you personally feel you stand at this time? On which step do you think you will stand about five years from now?" Gallup has used this scale in its world poll covering more than 150 countries.

The third type of data, called eudaemonic information, tries to measure one's sense of purpose in life. Those who find reward in their work or in volunteering or altruism score well on these questions.

Well-being metrics gained prominence when they were better able to explain anomalies in social data that could not be explained by economic variables alone. Why, for example, were so many prime working age males in the United States dropping out of the workforce despite a booming economy? Why were there record numbers of suicides in India and China at the same time as these countries were enjoying rapid economic growth and historically unprecedented reductions in extreme poverty? The answers appeared to lie with subjective feelings that contradicted objective data on economic prosperity. Without a sense of purpose or community, the middle class was not feeling as if it was living the good life. The new metrics provided guides to what was going wrong.

Cross-disciplinary insights have also lent credibility to the importance of subjective data. One of the most striking findings of psychology is how much stronger the fear of loss is compared to the opportunity for gain. Nobel laureates Kahneman and Tversky pointed out that people value things they already have far more than others would be willing to pay for the same object. The gap is related to the fear of moving from the known situation to an unknown situation. The middle class tends to be very risk averse. It can cope with adversity, but it does not like instability and uncertainty. This may be why the middle class has taken up the causes of environmentalism and nature conservation so strongly. It is also why, in the past, it supported autocratic leaders who promised better times ahead. The combination of a message of hope and a plan to eliminate uncertainty, however flawed, can be a powerful antidote to feelings of a lack of control over the future.

The findings from psychology have been buttressed by biology. Humans crave social contact, and this behavior is associated with production of a hormone called oxytocin, which is produced in the hypothalamus. Oxytocin has been referred to as the "love hormone" because of its association with interpersonal bonding. But oxytocin has other functions. It has been linked with the human tendency toward parochial altruism: a willingness to self-sacrifice in the interests of one's own community, while simultaneously resisting threats from outside groups.[9] Oxytocin, in turn, stimulates anandamide in the nucleus accumbens and triggers the production of cannabinoid receptors that heighten motivation and happiness.[10] Thus there are direct physiological reasons why humans should embrace social interactions and altruistic behaviors, and therefore why measuring these outcomes is a core component of well-being.

Lower Stress and Work-Life Balance for the Middle Class

Of all the hedonic indicators of well-being—such as the extent of smiling, frowning, or feelings of anxiety or stress—it is stress that has the largest impact on people's lives. Chronic stress is a major impediment to the good life. It is associated with mental health problems—depression, anxiety, and insomnia—and with physical symptoms of pain, muscle tension, digestive issues, and even heart problems. Stress measurements are now a common feature on an archetypical middle-class product—the smartwatch.

Unfortunately, chronic stress is often associated with overwork. In the competitive modern economy, hard work is required in almost every job. For a generation that saw the pain of the Depression or World War II, working hard did not seem like something to complain about. For the middle class, it has become a badge of honor, a credo about how to get ahead and build a better life for oneself and one's family. This is taken so literally that the discussion of work-life imbalance usually treats it as a middle-class problem. In line with this thinking, the middle class is characterized as time poor, the lower class as income poor, while the rich have both enough income and enough time for leisure.

The middle-class imperative of working hard is taken to the extreme in some Asian cultures. In Japan, for example, employees are encouraged to work overtime, often amounting to eighty hours per week, and to socialize with their work colleagues after working hours to build camaraderie and a stronger corporate culture. The strain can mount. The Japanese have coined the term *karoshi* to signify death by overwork. An infamous case of twenty-four-year-old Matsuri Takahashi, who committed suicide on Christmas Day 2015 after regularly putting in one-hundred-hour weeks at the Dentsu advertising company, shocked the nation. Her simple last words: "Why do things have to be so hard?"

Japan is not alone. South Korea has a reputation for being the advanced economy with the longest average working hours. China is now seeing a campaign of *tang ping*, or "lying flat," among young graduates objecting to the "996" (9:00 a.m. to 9:00 p.m., six days a week) expectations of their employers. Hong Kong is often considered to be the city with the longest working hours. Indians topped the rankings of average hours worked in a 2016 Manpower study of nineteen thousand millennials across twenty-five countries. Long hours are pervasive no matter which country clocks the most.[11]

The insidious irony is that long hours do not always translate into greater output in a modern economy. There are surprisingly large differences in the average number of hours worked across countries. Europeans, in general, tend to work shorter hours, with German workers among the shortest of them all. This has come about thanks to pressures from unions, which have successfully fought for a maximum of forty-eight working hours per week. Now companies and governments themselves are finding that they need to counter the built-in culture of overwork by mandating time off and reducing formal working hours.

One of the largest experiments of this type has been conducted in Iceland. Between 2015 and 2019, the Reykjavik City Council and the Icelandic government gave three thousand workers a half day off each week (as well as the weekend) with no cut in their pay. According to the study authors, "productivity and service provision remained the same or improved across the majority of trial workplaces. Worker well-being increased across a range of indicators, from perceived stress and burnout to health and work-life balance."[12] Following the trials, unions in Iceland have pushed for reduced working hours, and by June 2021, 86 percent of the country's entire working population has reduced their hours or gained the right to do so.

The study findings may not be replicable in other countries. Iceland started with some of the longest working hours in Scandinavia, which left a sizable proportion of the workforce too tired to do regular household chores when returning home. With most of the population, men and women, working full time, this left many households feeling fatigued and stressed. Studies in other countries, however, have documented similar results, although they have not been conducted at the same size and have not led to the same kind of negotiated national changes in expected work schedules. France reduced its standard workweek to thirty-five hours in 2000 but did not stipulate that wages were not to be cut. Many French workers still are expected to work longer hours, and some are eligible for overtime pay for these extra hours. Thus, the French labor reforms have resulted in higher total labor compensation rather than a reduction in the average number of hours worked. France emerges in the middle of the pack among European countries in terms of the change in average hours worked per year between 2005 and 2015.

Work-life balance is a particular issue for women and a core element of gender inequality in society. Globally, women do almost three times as much unpaid domestic work as men.[13] In most middle-class societies, this imbalance is smaller than the global average but remains significant. Even when women work outside the home and contribute financially to household income, they also take on the bulk of time-consuming homemaking tasks, such as caring for children and other family members and household chores. As a result, women tend to sleep less and display greater degrees of stress. Gallup conducts a global poll called the Negative Experience Index. The 2020 results showed that women with children younger than fifteen years old were the "saddest, angriest, most worried and stressed out of all."[14]

It is hard for middle-class families to live the good life if they are stressed. Dual-earner families and single parents face major time shortages. There is some adaptation already happening, and the pace of change is likely to accelerate following the COVID-19 pandemic, which forced multiple experiments with alternative work arrangements. Already, Unilever New Zealand, Microsoft Japan, Shake Shack and Kickstarter in the United States, Elephant ventures in the Philippines, and Radioactive Public Relations in the United Kingdom are among companies that have moved to or experimented with four-day work-weeks. They uniformly find that employees take fewer sick days, stress levels decrease, time spent with families increases. Happier employees are more productive employees. Post-pandemic, flexibility on work conditions is helping companies attract the best talent. Market forces, the ultimate drivers of middle-class well-being, appear to be moving toward a new equilibrium with fewer hours at work.

The pandemic has accelerated the change because it has given the middle class a taste of greater freedom and control over their time—and the young generation in particular likes it. The new middle class of Gen Z may not be prepared to return to the nine-to-five routine (or the reality of far longer hours) of the traditional salaried office job. They are demanding greater flexibility. Whether they will succeed in changing the norms or be rebuffed by old-style corporate cultures remains an open question. For every company offering flexible work schedules, like American Express, there is another company like Goldman Sachs pushing back against such flexibility. It is a new battleground of the middle class against corporate interests.

Life Satisfaction and Status of the Middle Class

Middle-class individuals place considerable emphasis on autonomy, control, and personal growth. They tend to have high self-esteem based on these drivers. When asked about their level of satisfaction with life, both as it is and where they see themselves in the future, middle-class respondents are generally self-satisfied. One of their defining characteristics has been hope for the future. When the middle class is hopeful that things will get better, their life satisfaction tends to rise.

Hopeful people develop goals and pathways to achieve those goals. They are motivated and focused. If the pathway is not working, they are creative about finding alternatives. Clinical psychologists argue that hope helps people deal with stressful situations. There is considerable empirical evidence that hope and subjective well-being are closely related to each other. For the middle class, hope—either for oneself or for one's family—is a core element of life satisfaction.

Much of this is well known and commonly accepted. Politicians, for example, are used to framing issues in terms of the opportunities that are created—a message of hope—rather than in terms of the problems that people face. The malaise that currently affects the middle class in advanced economies seems to be driven primarily by lack of hope.

The drop in hopefulness is concentrated in rich countries. When responding to the Global Attitudes Survey conducted by the Pew Research Center in 2014, half the people in emerging and developing economies felt that when children in their country grew up, they would be better off financially than their parents. Only 28 percent of respondents in advanced economies felt the same way (the French being the gloomiest of the lot). Across the world, most people felt that success in life was being determined by forces outside of their control.

It is these forces that the middle class looks to the government to manage. Among the issues that are relevant to people's life satisfaction are the levels of unemployment, inflation, public debt, and inequality, as well as climate change and nature conservation and preservation. Most of these are trending in the wrong direction, causing significant angst and the decline in hope that the survey data reveal in advanced economies.

Inequality is seen as a major challenge almost everywhere. The few exceptions are Japan, Vietnam, and Bangladesh. Elsewhere, inequality in one form or another—racial, gender, sexual orientation—is a growing part of the social discourse everywhere in the world. When many countries are tackling the same problem, common solutions can emerge. For example, 130 countries agreed in 2022 to apply a minimum tax on multinational corporations, a global effort to ensure that large companies pay their fair share. The impact of this policy may be modest in terms of the impact on inequality in any given country, but the symbolism of forging collective action to address a common global problem is significant. It suggests that the presence of a sizable middle class in many large economies demanding "fairness" can lead to international cooperation despite differing contexts and starting points.

Climate change and worry over the degradation of the natural world are other outside attributes that are responsible for the declining hope among the middle class. Governments need to act collectively to solve these problems. It is helpful that most of the major carbon-emitting countries now have a large middle class pushing for action. For example, the United States and Europe have already made strong commitments to move to net zero carbon emissions. China, too, has made significant commitments based on the perceived advantages that a low-carbon transformation can provide to its own middle class. The greatest resistance, not surprisingly, comes from countries where the middle class is smaller and less wealthy—India, Indonesia, and South Africa—which also rely heavily on coal. There, a nuanced trade-off between adding to domestic middle-class wealth and adding to middle-class well-being must be made. With international financial support, these countries too are ready to decarbonize their economies.

For the evaluative measures of well-being—the degree to which people are satisfied with their lives—the role of government to manage the broad contours of society is large and growing. The spread of the middle class across the world makes it possible now to imagine collective action solutions that were simply not feasible earlier.

The Power of Purpose in the Middle Class

The eudaemonic concept—happiness achieved through meaning and purpose in life—is perhaps the least well-defined and most hotly contested component of well-being. There seems to be agreement that there must be some purpose to being human and moving toward that purpose is the path of the life well lived. According to Aristotle, the pursuit of eudaemonia is not just to act in a certain way, but to do this with virtue. And "of all forms of virtue, liberality is the best beloved. The liberal man gives from a noble motive and in a right spirit, i.e., he gives the right amount to the right persons and at the right time; also his giving is done with pleasure or without pain. He does not take from wrong sources, nor does he ask favors."[15]

Doing things in the right way, for the right reasons, at the right times produces the greatest individual well-being; a very modern concept of what the middle class strives for. Translated into today's context, much of the Aristotelian tradition can be seen in the development of sustainable brands and the growth of volunteerism and altruism.

For years now, some middle-class consumers have been voting with their pocketbooks, buying products that have some social value to the purchaser beyond the goods or services themselves. They add purpose to their economic choices and feel better for doing so. The movement toward purchasing organic or locally grown food is an example; fair trade coffee or patronizing independent bookstores are others. Some companies are explicit about using this as a business strategy. The apparel and accessories company Toms bills itself as "fashion for a good cause. We're in business to improve lives." Toms donates one-third of its profits for grassroots good. The German company Share has a similar philosophy. When you buy a product from Share, "every snack donates a meal, every care product a hygiene product, every drink a day of drinking water, and every stationery item donates a school lesson."

Toms and Share are just small examples of a larger trend. In a survey of business leaders in the United States, the consultancy firm PwC found that 79 percent of business leaders believe that purpose is central to their success, although the PwC analysts caution that fewer than half those leaders actually put this into practice when making decisions.[16] For the early adopters, it can be a leap of faith. CVS, the large US retail company, had revenues of about $2 billion per year from cigarette sales when it made a corporate decision in 2014 to rebrand its pharmacy department as CVS Health and end cigarette sales as incompatible with its new focus on health. The short-run losses in cigarette sales were more than made up by gains in sales in the pharmacy department.

Some companies move toward being purpose-driven as a defensive measure. Gen Zers (those born between the mid-1990s and the mid-2000s) have found that TikTok and other social media can be used effectively to campaign against companies (or individuals) that behave in inappropriate ways. They have used "cancel culture" to advance their values by harnessing their market power. They can also do so in positive ways. One survey in the United States revealed that half of all Gen Zers were positively influenced to buy from "a brand showing dedication to social impact, by giving proceeds to charity, being environmentally conscious, having strong values, or projecting an impact-driven image."[17]

Gen Zers want to work in purpose-driven companies. Two-thirds of them in the United States say they want to make the world a better place. And more than 90 percent think that a good way to do this is to work for a company with the right approach toward social and environmental issues. They then want to contribute to the company's goals and look for an empowering culture where, from the start of their careers, they can influence decisions. Labor markets are starting to adjust to this new normal.

Capital markets are also adapting. In 2022, the volume of sustainable bonds (bonds issued with a distinct social purpose) surpassed $2 trillion.[18] This is still a small fraction of the global bond market (around $130 trillion in 2022), but it represents a significant milestone. ESG (environment, social, and governance) bonds are the most rapidly growing segment of global capital markets, with sizable issuances in the United States, Europe, China, and South Korea. Problems abound in establishing proper definitions and criteria as to what qualifies as a sustainable bond and what does not (for example, should an energy company whose activities are powered primarily by fossil fuels be permitted to issue a green bond for a small renewables project?), but the reason for the explosion of this market is straightforward. Investors are looking for more than financial returns when they lend money to companies. They want to know the money is going to be used for a good purpose. Companies are simply tapping into this demand. And who are these investors? They are the middle class, aligning themselves with the wealthy, who need support to move the agenda on climate change, which could be an existential crisis for them.

All this may seem faddish and marginal, but it is gaining ground and becoming mainstream. "Net zero" started as an aspiration for governments to embark on a program for decarbonizing their economies. Credible net-zero strategies have a plan with long-term and intermediate targets, a well-articulated program of actions and activities, and a framework for monitoring achievements—a pledge, plan, proceed, and publish process. What is new is how fast this has morphed from the sphere of governments and policymakers into the realm of companies and boardrooms. A review of all the companies in the Forbes Global 2000 list shows that 417 of them, representing $14 trillion in annual sales, or one-third the total sales of the group, have already made a net zero commitment. Consumer-facing sectors in the households and personal products sector are even more committed, with more than two-thirds having net zero pledges. On the other hand, companies in aerospace and defense (10 percent) and business-to-business sectors (5 percent) have been slower to move.[19] The economic power of the middle class and its desire to include societal purpose in its economic choices is clear.

There is a similar desire to have purpose outside of work, largely through volunteering and altruism. Altruism, defined as behavior to help others without expectation of reward, has been systematically associated with higher life satisfaction, more happiness, and better health. The finding is robust across cultures. Individuals may, as we have seen, get rewarded through biochemical stimuli (prompting some academic debate as to whether such behavior should truly be classified as altruistic or not), but the "feel good" sensation associated with altruism is a strong motivator of behavior. So much so that in many populations, most people like to think of themselves as more altruistic than average.

Altruism and volunteering have become closely linked in the popular imagination with the middle class (often with middle-class women). Yet it is prevalent among all classes, rich and poor. Volunteering creates strong social relationships built through a shared endeavor, along with opportunities to self-organize in local communities. There is often a blurred line between volunteerism to build community resilience and collective action to tackle community problems together. According to the UN, volunteers accounted for 109 million full-time equivalent work years in 2016, about one-thirtieth of total global employment.[20] In other words, volunteering averages more than an hour a week for every worker in the world. Most of this is informal. Women do two-thirds of volunteer work in Latin America and North America, but in other regions there is a more even balance between genders. In Asia, men do more volunteering than women. Technology has opened up whole new avenues for cost-effective, just-in-time, online volunteering.

A New Middle-Class Narrative: From Consumerism to Well-Being

It is easy to become overwhelmed by global problems. Looking at the scale of challenges now confronting us, the world seems destined for a dystopian future. But, for two hundred years, the middle class has found a way to steer the national ship in the right direction, albeit with a few misdirected turns. It has done this in the widest range of cultures, age groups, and contexts. It can do so again. It is possible that this is an overly optimistic view of the world, yet as the journalist Tom Friedman has said, "pessimists are usually right and optimists are usually wrong, but all the great changes have been accomplished by optimists."[21]

The difference today is that change cannot occur one country at a time, as it has done throughout the history of the middle class. There are global problems requiring global solutions. The middle class needs to work across boundaries, but the middle class in the West, Asia, and other countries have different histories. There is debate within the established middle class in North America and Europe as to whether the expansion of the new middle class in Asia and other developing regions benefits or harms them and, conversely, a debate in Asia as to whether the materialism of the Western middle class is responsible for overstepping planetary boundaries. Within and across countries, there are legitimate questions about the degree to which the middle class should bear the burden of wide-scale economic transformation. Similarly, there are debates as to whether the advances of technology are good for the middle class or whether automation and artificial intelligence are damaging opportunities for good jobs. These questions and debates can be resolved through domestic and international dialogue and economic reforms. Then, if the material component of middle-class well-being in advanced economies is solved, as Keynes predicted almost one hundred years ago, the focus should be shifted to the other components of well-being that are lagging behind. Those other components—addressing issues of stress and overwork, hope for the future, and altruism, volunteerism and a sense of purpose—can be pursued through reimagining how businesses, labor markets, and capital markets work.

Striving for well-being is common to the middle class everywhere, and that should be the source of optimism for change in the world. The start of this book posed the question: "Should the next generation strive to enter the middle class?" The answer is yes. It is the middle class that will drive change in the world. The core of the new middle-class message to governments, businesses, and civic associations everywhere is: "Help us live the good life by designing policies, regulations, products, and partnerships that permit the attainment of adequate material consumption while also promoting the other attributes of the good life."

Without the support of the middle class, past efforts for global change have come to naught. For example, environmentalists were once portrayed as anti–middle class and anti–economic growth "tree-huggers." By broadening the dialogue to everyone within the middle class and building bridges between nature conservationists and preservationists, the coalitions for change have grown. The history of the middle class has long been one of seeking coalitions with others. It must now do this on a grand scale to preserve and improve its own way of life by pushing governments to take collective action on the major threats to middle-class well-being.

Governments in advanced countries have started down this path, spurred by a generation questioning the happiness of a traditional middle-class lifestyle. Businesses are now following suit, learning about how to attract younger members of the middle class to buy their products. Capital markets are following the lessons of successful companies. The direction of change is clear even if the pace is, as yet, insufficient to deal with the urgency for action.

This change in focus and narrative is welcome. Without it, the great global challenges of our time—climate change and nature conservation and preservation—would be left to a few well-meaning individuals. There is a reason why the environmental movement on its own struggled to gain a foothold in national politics for so long despite the merits of its cause: it simply did not have the mass appeal required. With vast numbers of the middle class now embracing these causes and recognizing the links with their own well-being, the chances of success increase. And because these causes are so fundamental to middle-class well-being throughout the world, the chances for collective action by governments and business are sharply improved.

ACKNOWLEDGMENTS

In 1985, I visited a poor fishing village in Kelantan, the poorest state of peninsular Malaysia. I was astonished to find a well-outfitted health clinic, TV antennas on all the houses, and a concrete jetty for landing and marketing the fish catch. Although classified as "poor" by the Malaysian authorities, the village looked closer to a middle-class community than to the poor communities I was used to seeing in my South Asian birthplace. This was the start of my fascination with defining the middle class, studying its emergence in developing countries, and thinking about the impact it was having in our world. Two decades later, I turned this fascination into an academic study of the global middle class published by the Organization of Economic Cooperation and Development (OECD), an international organization working to build policies for better lives. The data in this book draws from that work, which also describes the methodology behind the calculations.

Shortly thereafter, I had a chance encounter with the brilliant journalist and writer Moisés Naím, a former minister for development in Venezuela. When I described to him what I was working on, he replied, "This is not for academics; you should write a book for a general audience." That conversation was the seed for this work.

I realized, as I started to write, that I needed considerable help, not just with researching the topic, but with opening my eyes to the perspective of a younger generation, those who I hope will take up the mantle of using middle-class power to better the lives of everyone on the planet. Jasmin Baier volunteered her time, energy, intellect, and keen eye over many months in this role. I am so thankful and grateful for her enormous contribution.

My friends also pitched in to educate me. Surjit and Ravi Bhalla helped me understand India. Cheng Li reviewed the chapter on China. Carol Graham showed me how to link the middle class to happiness and the good life. David Garlock gave detailed comments on the narrative. David Gootnick gave feedback as a guinea pig "target audience." My family circle were cheerleaders when I needed it most. I am grateful to all of them.

Finally, I'd like to thank my editors, Bill Finan and Yelba Quinn, for believing in this project and for all their work in getting it over the finish line.

NOTES

Preface

1. Thomas Hobbes, *Leviathan*, ed. J. C. A. Gaskin (London: Oxford University Press, 2008).

2. Homi Kharas and Kristofer Hamel, "A Global Tipping Point: Half the World Is Now Middle Class or Wealthier," Brookings Institution, September 27, 2018, www.brookings.edu/blog/future-development/2018/09/27/a-global-tipping-point-half-the-world-is-now-middle-class-or-wealthier/.

3. Andrew T. Jebb, Louis Tay, Ed Diener, and Shigehiro Oishi, "Happiness, Income Satiation, and Turning Points around the World," *Nature Human Behaviour* 2, no, 1 (2018): 33–38, www.researchgate.net/publication/321743107_Happiness_Income_Satiation_and_Turning_Points_Around_the_World.

4. James Carville and Stan Greenberg, *It's the Middle Class, Stupid!* (New York: Plume, 2013).

5. "Growth and the Middle Class," *Democracy Journal* 20 (spring 2011), https://democracyjournal.org/magazine/20/growth-and-the-middle-class/; OECD, *Under Pressure: The Squeezed Middle Class* (Paris: OECD Publishing, 2019), www.oecd.org/els/soc/OECD-middle-class-2019-main-findings.pdf; Natalie Chun, Rana Hasan, Muhammad Habibur Rahman, and Mehmet Ali Ulubaşoğlu, "The Role of Middle Class in Economic Development: What Do Cross-Country Data Show?," *Review of Development Economics* (May 29, 2016), https://onlinelibrary.wiley.com/doi/abs/10.1111/rode.12265.

6. Ronald F. Inglehart and Christian Welzel, "How Development Leads to Democracy: What We Know about Modernization Today," *Foreign Affairs* 88, no. 2 (2009): 33–48, https://papers.ssrn.com/sol3/papers.cfm?abstract_id=2391678.

7. Tom W. Smith, Michael Davern, Jeremy Freese, and Stephen L. Morgan, General Social Surveys, 1972–2018, https://gss.norc.org/.

8. Anne Case and Angus Deaton, "Mortality and Morbidity in the 21st Century," Brookings Papers on Economic Activity, 2017.

9. Richard Reeves, "A Middle Class Theory of Relativity: 4 Benchmarks," Brookings Institution, April 10, 2019, www.brookings.edu/blog/up-front/2019/04/10/a-middle-class-theory-of-relativity-4-benchmarks/.

10. Eric Lonergan and Mark Blyth, *Angrynomics* (Newcastle: Agenda, 2020).

11. Seymour Martin Lipset, "Democracy and Working-Class Authoritarianism," *American Sociological Review* 24, no. 4 (1959), www.jstor.org/stable/2089536.

12. FRED Economic Data, "Personal Consumption Expenditures," St. Louis Fed, https://fred.stlouisfed.org/series/PCE, accessed March 17, 2023.

13. Jim Puzzanghera, "A Decade after the Financial Crisis, Many Americans Are Still Struggling to Recover," *Los Angeles Times*, September 9, 2018, www.latimes.com/business/la-fi-financial-crisis-middle-class-20180909-htmlstory.html; Don Peck, "Can the Middle Class Be Saved?," *The Atlantic*, September 2011, www.theatlantic.com/magazine/archive/2011/09/can-the-middle-class-be-saved/308600/.

14. Homi Kharas, "The Unprecedented Expansion of the Global Middle Class," Brookings Institution, Global Economy and Development Working Paper No. 100, February 2017, www.brookings.edu/wp-content/uploads/2017/02/global_20170228_global-middle-class.pdf.

Chapter 1. The Middling Sort

1. Bank of England Inflation Calculator: 1209–Present, www.bankofengland.co.uk/monetary-policy/inflation/inflation-calculator.

2. Vivian Song, "World's Oldest Department Store Feels Like the Streets of Paris," CNN Travel, March 10, 2020, https://edition.cnn.com/travel/article/le-bon-marche-paris-department-store/index.html.

3. John Morley, *The Life of Richard Cobden* (London: T. Fisher Unwin, 1879).

4. Thorstein B. Veblen, *The Theory of the Leisure Class: An Economic Study of Institutions* (London: Macmillan, 1899).

5. Charles Mackay, *Extraordinary Popular Delusions and the Madness of Crowds* (Wordsmith Reference, 1995).

6. *The Collected Works of John Stuart Mill*, vol. 23, *Newspaper Writings August 1831–October 1834, Part II*, ed. Ann P. Robson and John M. Robson (Toronto: University of Toronto Press, 1986).

7. Susan Carr, "In Search of the *Gentilhommes Campagnards:* Noble Diversity and Social Structure in Burgundy, 1682–1789 (St. Andrews, UK: Centre for French History and Culture, University of Saint Andrews, 2017).

8. John Forster, *The Life of Charles Dickens*, vols. 1–3 (Boston: James R. Osgood, 1875; Project Gutenberg, 2008).

9. Liza Picard, "The Victorian Middle Classes," British Library, October 14, 2009, www.bl.uk/victorian-britain/articles/the-victorian-middle-classes.

10. David Cannadine. "The Landowner as Millionaire: The Finances of the Dukes of Devonshire, c.1800–c. 1926," *The Agricultural History Review* 25, no. 2 (1977): 77–97, www.jstor.org/stable/40273888; Mark Rothery, "The Wealth of the English Landed Gentry, 1870–1935," *Agricultural History Review* 55, no. 2 (2007): 251–68.

11. Credit Suisse, "The Global Wealth Report 2021," Credit Suisse Research Institute, June 2021, www.credit-suisse.com/media/assets/corporate/docs/about-us/research/publications/global-wealth-report-2021-en.pdf.

12. *Financial Times*, "Nestle Cuts Africa Workforce as Middle Class Growth Disappoints," June 16, 2015, www.ft.com/content/de2aa98e-1360-11e5-ad26-00144feabdc0.

13. UK Inflation Calculator, Alioth Finance, November 21, 2022, www.officialdata.org/uk/inflation/1850?amount=1.

14. OECD, "National Accounts: 4. PPPs and Exchange Rates," https://stats.oecd.org/Index.aspx?DataSetCode=SNA_Table4, accessed December 1, 2022.

15. Henry Colin Gray Matthew, *Gladstone, 1809–1874* (Oxford: Clarendon Press, 1988), 127.

16. Cited in Stuart Blumin, *The Emergence of the Middle Class* (Cambridge: Cambridge University Press, 1989), 1.

17. Luis F. Lopez-Calva and Eduardo Ortiz-Juarez, "A Vulnerability Approach to the Definition of the Middle Class," Policy Research Working Paper No. WPS 5902, 2011, World Bank https://openknowledge.worldbank.org/handle/10986/3669.

18. Homi Kharas, "The Emerging Middle Class in Developing Countries," Organization of Economic Co-operation and Development Working Paper No. 285, 2010.

19. Isabella Beeton, *Mrs. Beeton's Book of Household Management* (1861; Project Gutenberg, 2003).

20. *Annual Report of the White House Task Force on the Middle Class*, February 2010, https://obamawhitehouse.archives.gov/sites/default/files/microsites/100226-annual-report-middle-class.pdf.

Chapter 2. The First Billion

1. Carl T. Lira, "Brief History of the Steam Engine," Michigan State University, www.egr.msu.edu/~lira/supp/steam/index.htm, accessed December 7, 2022.

2. Diego A. Comin and Marti Mestieri, "Technology Diffusion: Measurement, Causes and Consequences," in *Handbook of Economic Growth*, vol. 2, ed. Philippe Aghion and Steven Durlauf, 565–622 (North Holland: Elsevier, 2014).

3. Stafford H. Northcote and C. E. Trevelyan, *Report on the Organisation of the Permanent Civil Service Together with a Letter from the Rev. B. Jowett*, House of Commons (London: George E. Eyre and William Spottiswoode, for Her Majesty's Stationery Office, 1854), www.civilservant.org.uk/library/1854_Northcote_Trevelyan_Report.pdf

4. Henry Parris, "The Origins of the Permanent Civil Service, 1780–1830," *Public Administration* 46, no. 2 (1968): 143–66, https://onlinelibrary.wiley.com/doi/pdf/10.1111/j.1467-9299.1968.tb01357.x.

5. Erik Bengtsson and Svante Prado, "The Rise of the Middle Class: The Income Gap between Salaried Employees and Workers in Sweden, ca. 1830–1940," *Scandinavian Economic History Review* 68, no. 2 (2020): 91–111.

6. Elementary Education Act, 1876, www.educationengland.org.uk/documents/acts/1876-elem-educ-act.html and www.educationengland.org.uk/documents/acts/1893-elem-educ-blind-deaf-act.html.

7. Grace Chen, "A Relevant History of Public Education in the United States," *Public School Review*, February 17, 2021, www.publicschoolreview.com/blog/a-relevant-history-of-public-education-in-the-united-states.

8. Christelle Garouste, *100 Years of Educational Reforms in Europe: A Contextual Database*, JRC Scientific and Technical Reports, European Commission (Luxembourg, Publication Office of the European Union, 2010), https://publications.jrc.ec.europa.eu/repository/bitstream/JRC57357/reqno_jrc57357.pdf.

9. Max Roser, Hannah Ritchie, and Bernadeta Dadonaite, "Child and Infant Mortality," *Our World in Data*, 2013, https://ourworldindata.org/child-mortality.

10. "Population by World Region, including UN Projections," *Our World in Data*, https://ourworldindata.org/grapher/world-population-by-world-regions-post-1820, accessed December 12, 2022.

11. Leah Platt Bouston, Devin Bunton, and Owen Hearey, "Urbanization in the United States, 1800–2000," National Bureau of Economic Research Working Paper 19041, May 2013, https://scholar.princeton.edu/sites/default/files/lboustan/files/research21_urban_handbook.pdf.

12. Hannah Ritchie and Max Roser, "Urbanization," *Our World in Data*, September 2018, https://ourworldindata.org/urbanization.

13. Julia Zinkina, Ilya Ilyin, and Andrey Korotayev, "The Nineteenth-Century Urbanization Transition in the First World," *Globalistics and Globalization Studies* (2017): 164–72.

14. Alexis C. Madrigal, "Germans Used to Drink an Astounding Amount of Beer," *The Atlantic,* October 22, 2012, www.theatlantic.com/international/archive/2012/10/germans-used-to-drink-an-astounding-amount-of-beer/263944/.

15. Cissie Fairchilds, "Review: Consumption in Early Modern Europe. A Review Article," *Comparative Studies in Society and History* 35, no. 4 (1993): 850–58.

16. Lorna Weatherill, *Consumer Behavior and Material Culture in Britain, 1660–1760* (London: Routledge, 1996).

17. "Victorians: Daily Life," *English Heritage*, www.english-heritage.org.uk/learn/story-of-england/victorian/daily-life/, accessed December 16, 2022.

18. Francis Fukuyama, *Political Order and Political Decay: From the Industrial Revolution to the Globalization of Democracy* (New York: Farrar, Strauss and Giroux, 2014).

19. Bela Kun, "Marx and the Middle Classes," 1918, www.marxists.org/archive/kun-bela/1918/05/04.htm.

20. Asa Briggs, "Middle Class Consciousness in English Politics, 1780–1846," *Past & Present* 9, no. 1 (1956): 65–74, https://doi.org/10.1093/past/9.1.65.

21. Paul MacKendrick, Deno J. Geanakoplos, J. H. Hexter, and Richard Pipes, *Western Civilization: Paleolithic Man to the Emergence of European Powers* (New York: Harper & Row, 1968).

22. Jim Powell, "Thomas Babington Macaulay: Extraordinary Eloquence for Liberty," Foundation for Economic Education, October 1, 1996, https://fee.org/articles/thomas-babington-macaulay-extraordinary-eloquence-for-liberty/.

23. Cobden to Peel, June 23, 1846, quoted in Briggs, "Middle Class Consciousness in English Politics."

24. *First Report of the Commissioners Appointed to Inquire into the Municipal Corporations in England and Wales* (London: C. Knight, 1835), 49, https://catalog.hathitrust.org/Record/008604348.

25. "A New American Consumer Culture," US History II, https://courses.lumenlearning.com/suny-ushistory2os2xmaster/chapter/a-new-american-consumer-culture/, accessed December 16, 2022.

26. Roland Marchand, *Advertising the American Dream* (Berkeley: University of California Press, 1985).

27. Cited in Thomas C. Leonard, "Eugenics and Economics in the Progressive Era," *Journal of Economic Perspectives* 19, no. 4 (2005): 207–24, www.princeton.edu/~tleonard/papers/retrospectives.pdf.

28. Daniel T. Rodgers, "The Progressive Era to the New Era, 1900–1929," The Gilder Lehrman Institute of American History, https://ap.gilderlehrman.org/essays/progressive-era-new-era-1900-1929, accessed December 16, 2022.

29. Laura Root, "'Temporary Gentlemen' on the Western Front: Class Consciousness and the British Army Officer, 1914–1918," *Osprey Journal of Inquiry and Ideas* 5 (2006), https://digitalcommons.unf.edu/cgi/viewcontent.cgi?article=1071&context=ojii_volumes.

30. Matteo Battistini, "Middle Class, Classe Moyenne, Mittelstand: History and Social Sciences in the Atlantic World," in *Modern European-American Relations in the Transatlantic Space*, ed. by Maurizio Vaudagna (Torino: Otto Editore, 2015).

31. Klaus-Peter Sick, "Le Concept de Classes Moyennes: Notion Sociologique ou Slogan Politique," *Vingtieme Siecle. Revue d'histoire* 37 (1993): 13–33.

32. J. Artur, 1929, cited in Sick, "Le Concept de Classes Moyennes."

33. Seymour Martin Lipset, *Political Man: The Social Bases of Politics* (Garden City, NY: Doubleday, 1960).

34. Thomas Childers, *The Nazi Voter* (Chapel Hill: University of North Carolina Press, 1983).

35. Erich Fromm, *The Fear of Freedom* (London: Routledge, 1942).

36. Timothy W. Mason, "Some Origins of the Second World War," in *Nazism, Fascism and the Working Class*, ed. Timothy Mason and Jane Caplan (Cambridge: Cambridge University Press, 1995).

37. James Truslow Adams, *The Epic of America* (Boston: Little, Brown, 1931).

38. Stephen Kemp Bailey, *Congress Makes a Law: The Story behind the Employment Act of 1946* (New York: Columbia University Press, 1950).

39. Bailey, *Congress Makes a Law*.

40. Mark Twain and Charles Dudley Warner, *The Gilded Age: A Tale of Today* (Hartford, CT: The American Publishing Company, 1902), based on a manuscript deposited at the Library of Congress in 1873.

41. *The Graduate*, 1967, directed by Mike Nichols.

42. Christopher J. Tassava, *The American Economy during World War II*, The Economic History Association, https://eh.net/encyclopedia/the-american-economy-during-world-war-ii/, accessed December 19, 2022.

43. Quote Investigator, 2011, https://quoteinvestigator.com/2011/11/16/robots-buy-cars/.

44. Lizabeth Cohen, *A Consumer's Republic: The Politics of Mass Consumption in Postwar America* (New York: Vintage Books, 2004).

45. Wendell Cox and Jean Love, *The Best Investment a Nation Ever Made: A Tribute to the Dwight D. Eisenhower System of Interstate and Defense Highways* (Collingdale, PA: Diane Publishing, 1998).

46. John Kenneth Galbraith, *The Affluent Society* (Boston: Houghton Mifflin, 1958).

47. William Beveridge, *Social Insurance and Allied Services* (London: His Majesty's Stationery Office, 1992).

48. History, "Beetle Overtakes Model T as World's Best Selling Car," February 17, 1972, www.history.com/this-day-in-history/beetle-overtakes-model-t-as-worlds-best-selling-car#:~:text=On%20February%2017%2C%201972%2C%20the,production%20from%201908%20to%201927.

49. Organization for Economic Co-operation and Development, Statistics, Labour, Collective Bargaining Coverage, https://stats.oecd.org/Index.aspx?DatasetCode=STLABOUR#, accessed December 19, 2022.

Chapter 3. The Second Billion

1. Robert J. Lucas Jr., "On the Mechanics of Economic Growth," *Journal of Monetary Economics* 22, no. 1 (July 1988): 3–42.

2. Ricardo Hausmann, César A. Hidalgo, Sebastián Bustos, Michele Coscia, Alexander Simoes, and Muhammed A. Yildirim, *The Atlas of Economic Complexity* (Cambridge, MA: MIT Press, 2003).

3. Katelynn Harris, "Forty Years of Falling Manufacturing Employment," US Bureau of Labor Statistics, Employment and Unemployment, November 2020, www.bls.gov/opub/btn/volume-9/forty-years-of-falling-manufacturing-employment.htm.

4. IKEA, "The IKEA Vision and Values," accessed December 20, 2022.

5. Max Roser and Esteban Ortiz-Ospina, "Global Education," 2016, *Our World in Data*, https://ourworldindata.org/global-education.

6. Laura Edgehill, "Why Do South Koreans Teachers Get the Rock Star Treatment?," *World*, October 12, 2015, https://world.wng.org/2015/10/why_do_south_korean_teachers_get_the_rock_star_treatment.

7. Unpublished background paper for a conference held by the Institute for International Economics, Washington, DC, as cited in John Williamson, "The Strange History of the Washington Consensus," *Journal of Post Keynesian Economics* 27, no. 2 (2004): 195–206.

8. Williamson, "The Strange History of the Washington Consensus."

9. John Williamson, "Did the Washington Consensus Fail?," outline of speech at the Center for Strategic & International Studies, Washington, DC, Peterson Institute for International Economics, November 6, 2002.

10. Jaana Remes, Andrés Cadena, Alberto Chaia, Vijay Gosula, Jacques Bughin, James Manyika, Jonathan Woetzel, Nicolás Grosman, Tilman Tacke, and Kevin Russell, *Latin America's Missing Middle* (McKinsey Global Institute, 2019).

11. Indermit S. Gill and Martin Raiser, *Golden Growth: Restoring the Lustre of the European Economic Model*, The World Bank, 2012, https://documents1.worldbank.org/curated/en/539371468036253854/pdf/Main-report.pdf.

12. Stanley Fischer and Ratna Sahay, "Taking Stock," *Finance & Development*, September 2000, www.imf.org/external/pubs/ft/fandd/2000/09/pdf/fischer.pdf.

13. Jennifer Hunt, "Post-Unification Wage Growth in East Germany," National Bureau of Economic Research Working Paper No. 6878, January 1999.

14. Stephen Beard, "Itemizing Germany's $2 Trillion Bill for Reunification," *Marketplace*, November 5, 2019, www.marketplace.org/2019/11/05/itemizing-germanys-2-trillion-bill-for-reunification/.

15. Peter Bofinger, "The German Monetary Unification (GMU): Converting Marks to D-Marks," *Federal Reserve Bank of St. Louis Review* 72, no. 4 (July/August 1990), https://files.stlouisfed.org/files/htdocs/publications/review/90/07/German_Jul_Aug1990.pdf.

Chapter 4. The Third Billion

1. Ai Guo Han, "Building a Harmonious Society and Achieving Individual Harmony," *Journal of Chinese Political Science* 13, no. 2 (2008).

2. George H. W. Bush, "Remarks at the Yale University Commencement Ceremony in New Haven, Connecticut," May 27, 1991.

3. Qiang Fu, "The Persistence of Power Despite the Changing Meaning of Homeownership," *Urban Studies* 53, no. 6 (2016).

4. Lu Gao, "Achievements and Challenges: 30 Years of Housing Reform in the People's Republic of China," Asian Development Bank Working Paper No. 198, April 2010, www.adb.org/sites/default/files/publication/28408/economics-wp198.pdf.

5. EconData, CEIC China database, https://econdata.com/databases/ceic/#:~:text=CEIC%20China%20Database%20is%20a,and%20municipal%20data%20on%20China, accessed December 22, 2022.

6. Dennis Tao Yang, Junsen Zhang, and Shaojie Zhou, "Why Are Savings Rates So High in China?," National Bureau of Economic Research Working Paper No. 16771, February 2011, www.nber.org/papers/w16771.

7. Anthony Rush, "China's Labour Market," *Reserve Bank of Australia Bulletin*, September 2011, www.rba.gov.au/publications/bulletin/2011/sep/pdf/bu-0911-4.pdf.

8. John Knight and Jinjun Xue, "How High Is Urban Unemployment in China?," *Journal of Chinese Economic and Business Studies* 4, no. 2 (2006): 91–107.

9. Xin Meng, Chris Manning, Shi Li, and Tadjuddin Noer Effendi, *The Great Migration: Rural-Urban Migration in China and Indonesia* (Northampton: Edward Elgar Publishing, 2010).

10. Gilles Guiheux, "The Political 'Participation' of Entrepreneurs: Challenge or Opportunity for the Chinese Communist Party?," *Social Research* 73, no. 1 (2006).

11. David H. Autor, David Dorn, and Gordon H. Hanson, "The China Shock: Learning from Labor Market Adjustment to Large Changes in Trade," National Bureau of Economic Research Working Paper No. 21906, 2016, www.nber.org/papers/w21906.

12. Dorothy J. Solinger, "Labor Discontent in China in Comparative Perspective," *Eurasian Geography and Economics* 48, no. 4 (2007): 413–38.

13. M. Elfstrom and S. Kuruvilla, "The Changing Nature of Labor Unrest in China," *Industrial & Labor Relations Review* 67, no. 2 (2014): 453–80.

14. *The Economist*, "Light and Death: Suicides at Foxconn," May 29, 2010.

15. GETChina Insights, "China No. 1 on 2018 PISA: Is the Country Really an Education Powerhouse as the Rankings Suggest?," January 3, 2020, https://edtechchina.medium.com/china-1-on-2018-pisa-is-the-country-really-an-education-powerhouse-as-the-rankings-suggest-8b626cc1ae92.

16. Thomas L. Friedman, "The Shanghai Secret," *New York Times*, October 23, 2013, www.nytimes.com/2013/10/23/opinion/friedman-the-shanghai-secret.html.

17. Zhang Chunyan, Chen Jia, Wu Wencong, and Tang Yue, "Li Pledges Measures in Fight for Clean Air," *China Daily USA*, January 16, 2013, http://usa.chinadaily.com.cn/epaper/2013-01/16/content_16125844.htm.

18. Qiang Zhang, Yixuan Zheng, Dan Tong, and Jiming Hao, "Drivers of Improved PM2.5 Air Quality in China from 2013 to 2017," *PNAS* 116, no. 49 (2019), www.pnas.org/content/116/49/24463.

19. "Under the Dome by Chai Jing: Air Pollution in China," YouTube, March 8, 2015, www.youtube.com/watch?v=V5bHb3ljjbc.

20. Zhang Chun, "China Court Rules in Favour of First Public Interest Environmental Lawsuit," *China Dialogue*, November 11, 2015, https://chinadialogue.net/en/pollution/8291-china-court-rules-in-favour-of-first-public-interest-environmental-lawsuit/.

21. Zhe Liu, Anthony N. Mutukumira, and Hongjun Chen, "Food Safety Governance in China: From Supervision to Coregulation," *Food Science & Nutrition* 7, no. 12 (2019): 4127–39, www.ncbi.nlm.nih.gov/pmc/articles/PMC6924309/.

22. Anita Chang, "12 More Arrested in China's Tainted Milk Scandal," Associated Press, September 21, 2008.

23. Anne Case and Angus Deaton, "Rising Morbidity and Mortality in Midlife among White Non-Hispanic Americans in the 21st Century," *PNAS* 112, no. 49 (November 2, 2015), www.pnas.org/content/112/49/15078.

24. Raj Chetty, Nathaniel Hendren, Patrick Kline, Emmanuel Saez, "Where Is the Land of Opportunity? The Geography of Intergenerational Mobility in the United States," *Quarterly Journal of Economics* 129, no. 4 (November 2014).

25. Carol Graham and Sergio Pinto, "The Geography of Desperation in America," *Social Science & Medicine* 270 (February 2021), https://doi.org/10.1016/j.socscimed.2020.113612.

26. Danny Quah, "The Global Economy's Shifting Centre of Gravity," *Global Policy* 2, no. 1 (January 2021), https://onlinelibrary.wiley.com/doi/full/10.1111/j.1758-5899.2010.00066.x.

Chapter 5. The Fourth Billion

1. Anil Kumar Malhotra, *A Passion to Build: India's Quest for Offshore Technology, a Memoir* (Lulu.com, 2007).

2. EDP Staffing Services, "2000 Computer Industry Salary Survey," www.csus.edu/indiv/c/chingr/info/salaries2000.pdf, accessed December 22, 2022.

3. Statista, "Number of Mobile Cellular Subscriptions in India from 2000 to 2021," www.statista.com/statistics/498364/number-of-mobile-cellular-subscriptions-in-india/, accessed December 22, 2022.

4. Telecom Regulatory Authority of India, "Highlights of Telecom Subscription Data as on 31st December 2015," press release no. 15, 2016, www.trai.gov.in/sites/default/files/PR_No_15_TSD_December_15.pdf.

5. Pankaj Jaloti and Pari Natarajan, "The Growth and Evolution of India's Software Industry," *Communications of the ACM* 62, no. 11 (November 2019): 64–69, https://cacm.acm.org/magazines/2019/11/240381-the-growth-and-evolution-of-indias-software-industry/fulltext.

6. India Brand Equity Foundation, "Services," January 2021, www.ibef.org/uploads/industry/Infrographics/large/Services-Infographic-January-2021.pdf, accessed December 22, 2022.

7. R. Inglehart and C. Welzel, *Modernization, Cultural Change and Democracy: The Human Development Sequence* (New York: Cambridge University Press, 2005).

8. B. N. Ghosh, *Gandhian Political Economy: Principles, Practice and Policy* (Aldershot, Hampshire, UK: Ashgate Publishing, 2007).

9. Albert O. Hirschman, *Exit, Voice, and Loyalty: Responses to Decline in Firms, Organizations, and States* (Cambridge, MA: Harvard University Press, 1970).

10. Financial Express On-Line, "How Many People in India Actually Pay Tax? Income Tax Department Clarifies PM Modi's Claim," February 13, 2020, www.financialexpress.com/economy/how-many-people-in-india-actually-pay-tax-income-tax-department-clarifies-pm-modis-claim/1867332/.

11. World Health Organization, Global Health Expenditure Database, https://apps.who.int/nha/database, accessed March 17, 2023.

12. Government of India, Ministry of Finance, Department of Economic Affairs, Economic Division, *Economic Survey 2016–17*, January 2017.

13. Government of India, *Economic Survey 2016–17*, 51.

14. Manjeet Bhatia, ed., *Locating Gender in the New Middle Class in India* (Shimla: Indian Institute of Advanced Studies, 2017).

15. S. Dickey, "The Pleasures and Anxieties of Being in the Middle: Emerging Middle-Class Identities in Urban South India," *Modern Asian Studies* 46, no. 3 (2012): 559–99.

16. A. Krishna and D. Bajpai, "Layers in Globalizing Society and the New Middle Class in India," *Economic and Political Weekly* 50, no. 5 (2015).

17. Prabhat Jha, Maya A Kesler, Rajesh Kumar, Faujdar Ram, Usha Ram, Lukasz Aleksandrowicz, Diego G. Bassani, Shailaja Chandra, and Jayant K. Banthia, "Trends in Selective Abortions of Girls in India: Analysis of Nationally Representative Birth Histories from 1990 to 2005 and Census Data from 1991 to 2011," *The Lancet* 377, no. 9781 (2011).

18. U.S. Department of the Treasury, "About the CARES Act and the Consolidated Appropriations Act," https://home.treasury.gov/policy-issues/coronavirus/about-the-cares-act, accessed December 22, 2022.

19. 117th Congress, Public Law 117-2, American Rescue Plan Act of 2021, www.congress.gov/bill/117th-congress/house-bill/1319/text.

20. Swetha Totapally, Petra Sonderegger, Priti Rao, Jasper Gosselt, and Gaurav Gupta, *State of Aadhaar Report, 2019* (Dalberg, 2019), https://stateofaadhaar.in/assets/download/SoA_2019_Report_web.pdf?utm_source=download_report&utm_medium=button_dr_2019.

Chapter 6. The Fifth Billion

1. "Why Are People in Denmark So Happy?," https://denmark.dk/people-and-culture/happiness, accessed December 22, 2022.

2. David Rothkopf, *Superclass* (New York: Farrar, 2002), https://carnegieendowment.org/2008/03/24/superclass-global-power-elite-and-world-they-are-making-pub-20002.

3. Greta Thunberg, speech given at the UN Climate Summit, New York, September 23, 2019.

4. Brundtland Commission, *Report of the World Commission on Environment and Development: Our Common Future* (New York: UN, August 4, 1987), https://sustainabledevelopment.un.org/content/documents/5987our-common-future.pdf.

5. Anthropocene Working Group, "Results of Binding Vote by AWG," May 21, 2019, http://quaternary.stratigraphy.org/working-groups/anthropocene/.

6. Matthew C. Nisbet, "Communicating Climate Change: Why Frames Matter for Public Engagement," *Environment: Science and Policy for Sustainable Development* 51, no. 2 (2009): 12–23.

7. Diana Ivanova, John Barrett, Dominik Wiedenhofer, Biljana Macura, Max Callaghan, and Felix Creutzig, "Quantifying the Potential for Climate Change Mitigation of Consumption Options," *Environment Research Letters* 15, no. 9 (2020), https://iopscience.iop.org/article/10.1088/1748-9326/ab8589.

8. Economist Intelligence Unit, "Energy Transition Will Move Slowly over the Next Decade," December 1, 2022, www.eiu.com/n/energy-transition-will-move-slowly-over-the-next-decade/#:~:text=By%202032%2C%20fossil%20fuels%20will,by%20the%20war%20in%20Ukraine.

9. IEA, "Net Zero by 2050: A Roadmap for the Global Energy Sector," 2021, https://iea.blob.core.windows.net/assets/4719e321-6d3d-41a2-bd6b-461ad2f850a8/NetZeroby2050-ARoadmapfortheGlobalEnergySector.pdf.

10. IEA, "Net Zero by 2050," 20.

11. Julio Friedman, Zhiyuan Fan, and Ke Tang, *Low Carbon Heat Solutions for Heavy Industry* (New York: Center on Global Energy Policy, 2019), www.energypolicy.columbia.edu/research/report/low-carbon-heat-solutions-heavy-industry-sources-options-and-costs-today.

12. https://climatecommunication.yale.edu/.

13. IEA, "Net Zero by 2050."

14. Green Eatz, "Food's Carbon Footprint," www.greeneatz.com/foods-carbon-footprint.html#:~:text=Food's%20Carbon%20Footprint%3A%20Eat%20vegetarian&text=A%20vegan%20diet%20has%20the,such%20as%20beef%20and%20lamb, accessed December 28, 2022.

15. United Nations, Department of Economic and Social Affairs, Statistics Division, "Responsible Consumption and Production," https://unstats.un.org/sdgs/report/2019/goal-12/, accessed December 28, 2022.

16. Silpa Kaza, Lisa Yao, Perinaz Bhada-Tata, and Frank Van Woerden, *What a Waste 2.0: A Global Snapshot of Solid Waste Management to 2050* (Washington, DC: World Bank, 2018), https://datatopics.worldbank.org/what-a-waste/trends_in_solid_waste_management.html.

17. World Bank, *Squaring the Circle: Policies from Europe's Circular Economy Transition, 2022* (Washington, DC: World Bank, 2022), www.worldbank.org/en/region/eca/publication/squaring-circle-europe-circular-economy-transition.

18. European Commission, *Directive on Single-Use Plastics*, July 2, 2019, https://ec.europa.eu/environment/topics/plastics/single-use-plastics_en.

19. IPBES, *The Global Assessment Report on Biodiversity and Ecosystem Services* (Bon, Germany: IPBES, 2019), https://ipbes.net/sites/default/files/inline/files/ipbes_global_assessment_report_summary_for_policymakers.pdf.

20. G. Ceballos, Paul R. Ehrlich, and Peter H. Raven, "Vertebrates on the Brink as Indicators of Biological Annihilation and the Sixth Mass Extinction," *PNAS* 117, no 24 (2020): 13596–602, https://doi.org/10.1073/pnas.1922686117.

21. Ceballos, Ehrlich, and Raven, "Vertebrates on the Brink."

22. Hannah Ritchie, "If the World Adopted a Plant-Based Diet We Would Reduce Global Agricultural Land Use from 4 to 1 Billion Hectares," Our World in Data, March 4, 2021, https://ourworldindata.org/land-use-diets.

23. World Resources Institute, *Atlas of Forest and Landscape Restoration Opportunities*, 2004, www.wri.org/data/atlas-forest-and-landscape-restoration-opportunities.

24. E. Dinerstein, C. Vynne, E. Sala, A. R. Joshi, S. Fernando, T. E. Lovejoy, J. Mayorga, D. Olson, G. P. Asner, J. E. M. Baillie, N. D. Burgess, K. Burkart, R. F. Noss, Y. P. Zhang, A. Baccini, T. Birch, N. Hahn, L. N. Joppa, and E. Wikramanayake, "A Global Deal for Nature: Guiding Principles, Milestones and Targets," *Science Advances* 5, no. 4 (2019), https://advances.sciencemag.org/content/5/4/eaaw2869#ref-16.

25. Sitala Peek, "Knocker Uppers: Waking Up the Workers in Industrial Britain," BBC News, March 27 2016, www.bbc.com/news/uk-england-35840393.

26. Genesis 1:28.

27. The Lutheran World Federation, *Dignity of Work: Theological and Interdisciplinary Perspectives* (Minneapolis, MN: Lutheran University Press, 2011).

28. United Nations, "Universal Declaration of Human Rights," December 10, 1948, www.un.org/en/about-us/universal-declaration-of-human-rights.

29. John Paul II, *Laborem exercens*, Encyclicals, September 14, 1981, www.vatican.va/content/john-paul-ii/en/encyclicals/documents/hf_jp-ii_enc_14091981_laborem-exercens.html.

30. John Paul II, "*Laborem exercens*."

31. *The Economist*, "What If an AI Won the Nobel Prize for Medicine?," July 3, 2021.

32. International Monetary Fund, *World Economic Outlook: Slowing Growth, Rising Risks* (Washington, DC: International Monetary Fund, 2011), www.imf.org/en/Publications/WEO/Issues/2016/12/31/Slowing-Growth-Rising-Risks.

33. Jan Mischke, Jonathan Woetzel, Sven Smit, James Manyika, Michael Birshan, Eckart Windhagen, Jörg Schubert, Solveigh Hieronimus, Guillaume Dagorret, and Marc Canal Noguer, *Will Productivity and Growth Return after the COVID-19 Crisis?* (McKinsey Global Institute, 2021), www.mckinsey.com/industries/public-and-social-sector/our-insights/will-productivity-and-growth-return-after-the-covid-19-crisis.

34. Marcela Escobari, Ian Seyal, and Carlos Daboín Contreras, "Moving Up: Promoting Workers' Economic Mobility Using Network Analysis," Brookings Institution, June 14, 2021.

35. Peterson Institute for International Economics, *How to Fix Economic Inequality* (Washington, DC: Peterson Institute for International Economics, 2020), www.piie.com/sites/default/files/documents/how-to-fix-economic-inequality.pdf.

36. Peterson Institute for International Economics, "How to Fix Economic Inequality," 7.

37. D. Acemoglu and D. Autor, "Skills, Tasks and Technologies: Implications for Employment and Earnings," in *Handbook of Labor Economics*, vol. 4 (North Holland, Amsterdam: Elsevier, 2010).

38. Hans Moravec, *Mind Children* (Cambridge, MA: Harvard University Press, 1988).

39. J. Kates-Harbeck, Alexey Svyatkovskiy, and William Tang, "Predicting Disruptive Instabilities in Controlled Nuclear Fusion Plasmas through Deep Learning," *Nature* 568 (2019): 526–31.

Chapter 7. A New Agenda for the Global Middle Class

1. John Maynard Keynes, "Economic Possibilities for Our Grandchildren (1930)," in *Essays in Persuasion* (New York: Harcourt Brace, 1932), 358–73.

2. Keynes, "Economic Possibilities for Our Grandchildren (1930)."

3. Richard A. Easterlin, Laura Angelescu McVey, Malgorzata Switek, Onnicha Sawangfa, and Jacqueline Smith Zweig, "The Happiness-Income Paradox Revisited," *PNAS* 107, no. 52 (2010): 22463–68.

4. Richard A. Easterlin, "Will Raising the Incomes of All Raise the Happiness of All?," *Journal of Economic Behavior and Organization* 27, no. 1 (1995).

5. Daniel Kahneman and Angus Deaton, "High Income Improves Evaluation of Life but Not Emotional Well-Being," *PNAS* 107, no. 38 (2010): 16489–93.

6. Liz Mineo, "Good Genes Are Nice but Joy Is Better," *Harvard Gazette*, April 11, 2017.

7. John F. Helliwell, Richard Layard, Jeffrey D. Sachs, Jan-Emmanuel De Neve, Lara B. Aknin, and Shun Wang, *World Happiness Report, 2021* (New York: United Nations, 2021), https://happiness-report.s3.amazonaws.com/2021/WHR+21.pdf.

8. Carol Graham and Sara MacLennan, "Policy Insights from the New Science of Well-Being," *Behavioral Science and Policy* 6, no. 1 (2020).

9. Carsten K. W. De Dreu, Lindred L. Greer, Michel J. J. Handgraaf, Shaul Shalvi, Gerben A. Van Kleef, Matthijs Baas, Femke S. Ten Velden, Eric Van

Dijk, and Sander W. W. Feith, "The Neuropeptide Oxytocin Regulates Parochial Altruism in Intergroup Conflict amongst Humans," *Science* 328, no. 5984 (2010): 1408–11.

10. University of California at Irvine, "'Love Hormone' Oxytocin Helps Produce 'Bliss Molecule' to Boost Pleasure of Social Interactions," *Social Psychology*, October 26, 2015.

11. ManpowerGroup, *Millennial Careers: 2020 Vision: Facts, Figures and Practical Advice from Workforce Experts* (ManpowerGroup, 2016), https://web.archive.org/web/20180314183158/https://www.manpowergroup.com.au/documents/White-Papers/2016_Millennials_2020Vision_White Paper.pdf.

12. Gudmundur D. Haraldsson and Jack Kellam, *Going Public: Iceland's Journey to a Shorter Working Week* (Alda, Association for Democracy and Sustainability and Autonomy, 2021), https://autonomy.work/wp-content/uploads/2021/06/ICELAND_4DW.pdf.

13. UN Women, *Turning Promises into Action: Gender Equality in the 2030 Agenda for Sustainable Development* (United Nations, 2018), www.unwomen.org/en/digital-library/publications/2018/2/gender-equality-in-the-2030-agenda-for-sustainable-development-2018.

14. Julie Ray, "2020 Another Emotionally Taxing Year for Women with Children," Gallup, 2021.

15. Aristotle, *The Nichomachean Ethics*, trans. J. E. C. Welldon (New York: Macmillan, 1902).

16. PwC, *Putting Purpose to Work* (PwC, June 2016), www.pwc.com/us/en/about-us/corporate-responsibility/assets/pwc-putting-purpose-to-work-purpose-survey-report.pdf.

17. "What Does a Purpose Driven Company Look Like?," Salesforce.org, 2019, www.salesforce.org/blog/what-does-a-purpose-driven-company-look-like.

18. "Green Bond Market Hits USD2tn Milestone at End of Q3 2022," Climate Bonds Initiative, September 11, 2022.

19. Energy and Climate Intelligence Unit and Oxford Net Zero, *Taking Stock: A Global Assessment of Net Zero Targets* (Energy and Climate Intelligence Unit and Oxford Net Zero, March 2021), https://ca1-eci.edcdn.com/reports/ECIU-Oxford_Taking_Stock.pdf?v=1616461369.

20. UN Volunteers, *The Thread That Binds: Volunteerism and Community Resilience* (UN Volunteers, 2018), www.unv.org/sites/default/files/UNV_SWVR_2018_English_WEB.pdf.

21. Thomas L. Friedman, AllAuthor.com, accessed May 04, 2023.

INDEX

ABOUT THE AUTHOR

Homi Kharas is a senior fellow at the Brookings Institution and a co-founder of World Data Lab, a company with a mission to make everyone count. An economist by training, he is a pioneer in the study of the global middle class. He has over four decades of experience working in or writing about international financial institutions, and he contributed to the shaping of the UN-brokered global agreement in 2015 to pursue Sustainable Development Goals in every country and region of the world. He has worked and traveled in almost ninety countries.